The
End of the
Roman Empire

PROBLEMS IN
EUROPEAN CIVILIZATION

The
End of the
Roman Empire

Decline or Transformation?
Second Edition

Edited and with an introduction by

Donald Kagan

Yale University

#124

D. C. HEATH AND COMPANY

Lexington, Massachusetts Toronto

CONTENTS

I THE PROBLEM OF DECLINE AND FALL STATED

II THE CAUSES

III NOT DECLINE BUT TRANSFORMATION

IV LESSONS FOR THE FUTURE

INTRODUCTION

Among the historical questions that have been posed through the ages, none has attracted more attention over a longer period of time than the one which asks, Why did the Roman Empire in the West collapse? It has remained a vital question because each age has seen in the tale of Rome's fall something significant and relevant to its own situation. The theme has been especially attractive in our own time; the fate of Rome looms large in the cosmic speculation of Spengler and Toynbee and has been intensively treated from countless points of view. The first treatment of the decline of Rome as an historical problem had to wait until the Renaissance when the Humanists became aware of their own break with the medieval period and, therefore, of the break between the Middle Ages and classical antiquity. Whether they blamed internal failures, as did Petrarch, or the barbarian attacks, as did Machiavelli, they were the first to show awareness of the problem.

An attempt is made to define the problem in Part I. The selection from M. Rostovtzeff divides the concept of decline into two major divisions: political, economic, and social decline on the one hand, and intellectual and spiritual on the other. For him the Roman Empire's decline meant the barbarization of political institutions, the simplification and localization of economic functions, the decay and disappearance of urban life, and, in the intellectual and spiritual sphere, the development among the masses of a mentality "based exclusively on religion and not only indifferent but hostile to the intellectual achievements of the higher classes." F. W. Walbank helps clarify the problem by setting it in its historical perspective and by defining the field of inquiry proper to it: "When we say a society is in decay, we refer to something having gone wrong within its structure, or in the relationship between the various groups which compose it."

A. H. M. Jones sees the problem in more simple, material terms and calls attention to the survival of the eastern half of the empire a millennium after the collapse in the West.

In Part II a selection of some of the explanations that have been offered for Rome's decay and collapse are presented. A glance at them will reveal the great variety of ways of viewing the problem and the forbidding difficulties standing in the way of a consensus. To begin with, the usual categories of explanation—political, economic, social, or moral—prove none too helpful, for all played some role, and rare is the explanation that fixes on one to the total exclusion of all others. Thus, A. E. R. Boak's thesis explaining the decline and fall of Rome in terms of manpower shortage is no less economic than it is social, and it has obvious political and moral facets as well. In the same way, the Rostovtzeff thesis employs all these categories to make its point of the barbarization of Rome by the absorption of the educated classes by the masses.

It may, therefore, be more useful to classify the solutions differently. Let students of Rome's decline imagine themselves as medical examiners who have been confronted with a corpse. It is their duty first to establish the time of death and then the cause. It soon becomes apparent that the various historical practitioners who have examined the Roman remains have achieved remarkably little agreement on either question. The general view has been that Rome reached its peak in the second century of the Christian era under its Antonine monarchs; it grew ill during the upheavals of the third century, suffered hardening of the arteries during the reforms of Diocletian and Constantine, and died under the onslaught of the barbarian tribes in the fifth century. The gravestone was laid in A.D. 476 when the last claimant to the Roman throne in the West was deposed, and that date was for long taken to be the boundary between antique and medieval society. This orthodox view was rudely challenged by Henri Pirenne, who, in the 1920s, asserted that the Roman Empire survived in all its essentials until the coming of Islam destroyed the unity of the Mediterranean and ended the Roman world.[1] At the other extreme is the view of Walbank—who finds the germs of the illness of antiquity already present in Athens in the fifth century B.C.—which suggests, in effect, that Rome had begun to die

[1] See Alfred F. Havighurst, *The Pirenne Thesis* (1976), another title in the "Problems in European Civilization" series.

before her empire had been born. Between these extremes is the view, held by Westermann among others, that the empire was really dead by A.D. 300, and it was only a ghostly apparition that the barbarians buried.

However little agreement there may be as to the time of Rome's demise, there is still less as to its cause. There are, perhaps, four applicable categories: death by accident, natural causes, murder, or suicide, and each is represented in these selections. The case for accidental death is made by J. B. Bury, who rejects all general causes. The theory of death from natural causes numbers Gibbon, Boak, and Walbank among its adherents, although each sees the victim succumbing to a different disease. The case for suicide has many advocates. Heitland, Westermann, MacMullen, and Rostovtzeff all believe that at some point Rome embarked on a policy that ultimately led to her destruction, but each fixes on a different policy as the culprit. Finally, there are those who believe that Rome fell by assassination. Baynes and Jones, by different paths, arrive at the conclusion that it was not a cadaver that fell to the German invaders, but a living organism they killed.

Nor are these the only aspects of the problem. For some the idea of decline and fall is itself inappropriate. These scholars point out that the inhabitants of the Roman world at the time of its collapse, though they complained of hard times, knew nothing about it, and that their immediate descendants seemed quite unaware of any great difficulties involved in an analysis of Rome's decline and fall. The fact is that "the decline and fall of the Roman Empire" is a metaphorical usage in which the empire is compared with an edifice; like all metaphors it conveys general impressions but not precise conceptions. The Roman Empire was not a building, but a complex system of government administration presiding over a vast area containing a very heterogeneous group of peoples and modes of life. These were held together by certain common institutions and by the power and skill of the Roman state. What does it mean to speak of the decline and fall of a set of relationships? The difficulty of the question has led some historians to abandon the concept of decline and fall altogether, and to speak rather of disintegration and transformation. For them the Roman Empire never fell at all, but was metamorphosed into something else. This is the subject of Part III. Peter Brown emphasizes the change in the geographic context of the world of late antiquity, while Ramsay MacMullen describes the change in its social character.

Still, though change may have been gradual and significant continuities did survive, there can be no doubt that the world of medieval Europe was radically different from that of the classical period—as different as the cathedral at Chartres is from the Parthenon in Athens or the Pantheon in Rome. It is, therefore, altogether proper to retain Gibbon's statement of the problem, for whenever and however the Roman world fell, there was a point at which it no longer stood. From the variety and multiplicity of the solutions offered, it may appear that no progress is possible in the search for understanding. In fact, the situation is not so bad as that, for most students of the problem first clear the field for their own interpretations by pointing out the shortcomings of other opinions. Thus, an important part of the selections presented herein is the careful criticism they offer of previous ideas. In this way, the less persuasive or altogether baseless theories may be weeded out and discarded.

Still, there will always remain a number of irreconcilable theories. A question of such scope and interest that it has remained vital for centuries is unlikely to find an answer satisfactory to everyone. Is it, then, useful or even meaningful to pose such a question as Why did Rome fall? Whatever the logical merits of the question, historians have always found it necessary to ask it, each generation framing it differently, each seeking answers along lines pertinent to its own needs. Certainly they have *thought* the question and its solution useful, for most have sought to draw lessons for the future from Rome's experience. Thus Part IV gives the views of five authors on the meaning of the decline and fall for their own and future generations. Whatever the merits of their conclusions, it is safe to guess that future historians will find them unsatisfactory and bring to the problem of Rome's collapse new ideas, deriving in part from the experience of their own age, while at the same time seeking light for their own problems emanating from the circumstances of Rome's fall.

Conflict of Opinion

The truth is that the success of the barbarians in penetrating and founding states in the western provinces cannot be explained by any general considerations. It is accounted for by the actual events and would be clearer if the story were known more fully. The gradual collapse of the Roman power in this section of the Empire was the consequence of *a series of contingent events.* No general cause can be assigned that made it inevitable.

—J. B. BURY

The decline of Rome was the natural and inevitable effect of immoderate greatness. Prosperity ripened the principle of decay; the causes of destruction multiplied with the extent of conquest; and, as soon as time or accident had removed the artificial supports, the stupendous fabric yielded to the pressure of its own weight. The story of its ruin is simple and obvious; and instead of inquiring why the Roman Empire was destroyed, we should rather be surprised that it had subsisted so long.

—EDWARD GIBBON

[The destructive tendencies of the Roman Empire arose] from the premises upon which classical civilization arose, namely an absolutely low technique and, to compensate for this, the institution of slavery. Herein lies the real cause of the decline and fall of the Roman Empire.

—F. W. WALBANK

With declining manpower and increasing impoverishment, the Roman Empire in the West, unable to defend itself against disintegration from within and invasion from without, staggered slowly on to its inevitable dissolution.

—A. E. R. BOAK

. . . It was the loss of economic freedom, even more than the loss of political freedom, which had such disastrous results upon private initiative and finally undermined Graeco-Roman civilization.

—W. L. WESTERMANN

We can hardly shut our eyes to the conclusion that a potent cause of the decline and fall of Rome is to be detected in the fatal absence of any nonrevolutionary means of reform.

—W. E. HEITLAND

The main phenomenon which underlies the process of decline is the gradual absorption of the educated classes by the masses and the consequent simplification of all the functions of political, social, economic, and intellectual life, which we call the barbarization of the ancient world.

—M. I. ROSTOVTZEFF

I have identified thirteen defects which, in my view, combined to reduce the Roman Empire to final paralysis. They display a unifying thread: the thread of *disunity*. Each defect consists of a specific disunity which split the Empire wide apart, and thereby damaged the capacity of the Romans to meet external aggressions. Heaven forbid that we ourselves should have a monolithic society without any internal disunities at all, or any differences of character or opinion. But there can arrive a time when such differences become so irreconcilably violent that the entire structure of society is imperiled. That is what happened among the ancient Romans. And that is why Rome fell.

—MICHAEL GRANT

The purpose of this book is to show how energies both harmonious and hostile to the Roman order appeared in a given class at a given time. As the locus of these energies moved down the social scale in the course of the first four centuries of the Empire, so the enemies of the state were, to begin with, drawn from senatorial ranks and, in the end, from peasants and barbarians. The drift of directing power outward and downward from the Roman aristocracy is well known; its corollary is the simultaneous movement of anti-Establishment impulses in the same direction.

—RAMSAY MACMULLEN

It was the increasing pressure of the barbarians, concentrated on the weaker western half of the empire, that caused the collapse.

—A. H. M. JONES

It was the pitiful poverty of Western Rome which crippled her in her effort to maintain that civil and military system which was the presupposition for the continued life of the ancient civilization.

—N. H. BAYNES

As the Mediterranean receded, so a more ancient world came to light. Small things sometimes betray changes more faithfully, because unconsciously. Near Rome, a sculptor's yard of the fourth century still turned out statues, impeccably dressed in the old Roman toga (with a socket for detachable portrait-heads!), but the aristocrats who commissioned such works would, in fact, wear a costume which betrayed prolonged exposure to the "barbarians" of the non-Mediterranean world—a woollen shirt from the Danube, a cloak from northern Gaul, fastened at the shoulders by a filigree brooch from Germany, even guarding their health by "Saxon" trousers. Deeper still, at the very core of the Mediterranean, the tradition of Greek philosophy had found a way of opening itself to a different religious mood.

Such changes as these are the main themes of the evolution of the Late Antique world.

—PETER BROWN

The Later Roman Empire

I THE PROBLEM OF DECLINE AND FALL STATED

Michael I. Rostovtzeff
THE DECAY OF ANCIENT CIVILIZATION

Michael I. Rostovtzeff, born in Kiev in 1870, was educated at the universities of Kiev and St. Petersburg. He was Professor of Latin and Roman History at St. Petersburg until the Communist revolution in 1918. He came to the United States in 1920 and took up a position at the University of Wisconsin. Five years later he was appointed Sterling Professor of Ancient History and Classical Archaeology at Yale, a position he held until his retirement. In 1935 he was president of the American Historical Association. Among his more outstanding contributions are The Social and Economic History of the Hellenistic World, *and* A History of the Ancient World.

Every reader of a volume devoted to the Roman Empire will expect the author to express his opinion on what is generally, since Gibbon, called the decline and fall of the Roman Empire, or rather of ancient civilization in general. I shall therefore briefly state my own view on this problem, after defining what I take the problem to be. The decline and fall of the Roman Empire, that is to say, of ancient civilization as a whole, has two aspects: the political, social, and economic on the one hand, and the intellectual and spiritual on the other. In the sphere of politics we witness a gradual barbarization of the Empire from within, especially in the West. The foreign, German, elements play the leading part both in the government and in the army, and settling-in masses displace the Roman population, which disappears from the fields. A related phenomenon, which indeed was a necessary consequence of this barbarization from within, was the gradual disintegration of the Western Roman Empire; the ruling classes in the former Roman provinces were replaced first by Germans and Sarmatians, and later by Germans alone, either through peaceful penetration or by conquest. In the East we observe a gradual orientalization of the Byzantine Empire, which leads ultimately to the establishment, on the ruins of the Roman Empire, of strong half-Oriental and purely Oriental states, the Caliphate of Arabia, and the Persian and Turkish empires. From the social and economic point of view, we mean by decline the gradual relapse of the ancient world to very primitive forms of economic life, into an almost pure "house-economy." The cities, which had created and sustained the higher forms of economic life, gradually decayed, and the majority of them practically disappeared from the face of the earth. A few, especially those that had been great centers of commerce and industry, still lingered on. The complicated and refined social system of the ancient Empire follows the same downward path and becomes reduced to its primitive elements: the king, his court and retinue, the big feudal landowners, the clergy, the mass of rural serfs, and small groups of artisans and merchants. Such is the political, social, and economic aspect of the problem. However, we must not generalize too much. The Byzantine Empire cannot be put on a level with the states of Western Europe or with the new Slavonic formations. But one thing is certain: on the ruins of the uniform economic life of the cities there began everywhere a special, locally differentiated, evolution.

From the intellectual and spiritual point of view the main phenomenon is the decline of ancient civilization, of the city-civilization of the Greco-Roman world. The Oriental civilizations were more stable: blended with some elements of the Greek city-civilization, they persisted and even witnessed a brilliant revival in the Caliphate of Arabia and in Persia, not to speak of India and China. Here again there are two aspects of the evolution. The first is the exhaustion of the creative forces of Greek civilization in the domains where its great triumphs had been achieved, in the exact sciences, in technique, in literature and art. The decline began as early as the second century B.C. There followed a temporary revival of creative forces in the cities of Italy, and later in those of the Eastern and Western provinces of the Empire. The progressive movement stopped almost completely in the second century A.D. and, after a period of stagnation, a steady and rapid decline set in again. Parallel to it, we notice a progressive weakening of the assimilative forces of Greco-Roman civilization. The cities no longer absorb—that is to say, no longer hellenize or romanize—the masses of the country population. The reverse is the case. The barbarism of the country begins to engulf the city population. Only small islands of civilized life are left, the senatorial aristocracy of the late Empire and the clergy; but both, save for a section of the clergy, are gradually swallowed up by the advancing tide of barbarism.

Another aspect of the same phenomenon is the development of a new mentality among the masses of the population. It was the mentality of the lower classes, based exclusively on religion and not only indifferent but hostile to the intellectual achievements of the higher classes. This new attitude of mind gradually dominated the upper classes, or at least the larger part of them. It is revealed by the spread among them of the various mystic religions, partly Oriental, partly Greek. The climax was reached in the triumph of Christianity. In this field the creative power of the ancient world was still alive, as is shown by such momentous achievements as the creation of the Christian church, the adaptation of Christian theology to the mental level of the higher classes, the creation of a powerful Christian literature and of a new Christian art. The new intellectual efforts aimed chiefly at influencing the mass of the population and therefore represented a lowering of the high standards of city-civilization, at least from the point of view of literary forms.

We may say, then, that there is one prominent feature in the development of the ancient world during the imperial age, alike in the political, social, and economic and in the intellectual field. It is a gradual absorption of the higher classes by the lower, accompanied by a gradual leveling down of standards. This leveling was accomplished in many ways. There was a slow penetration of the lower classes into the higher, which were unable to assimilate the new elements. There were violent outbreaks of civil strife: the lead was taken by the Greek cities, and there followed the civil war of the first century B.C. which involved the whole civilized world. In these struggles the upper classes and the city-civilization remained victorious on the whole. Two centuries later, a new outbreak of civil war ended in the victory of the lower classes and dealt a mortal blow to the Greco-Roman civilization of the cities. Finally, that civilization was completely engulfed by the inflow of barbarous elements from outside, partly by penetration, partly by conquest, and in its dying condition it was unable to assimilate even a small part of them.

The main problem, therefore, which we have to solve is this. Why was the city-civilization of Greece and Italy unable to assimilate the masses, why did it remain a civilization of the *élite*, why was it incapable of creating conditions which should secure for the ancient world a continuous, uninterrupted movement along the same path of urban civilization? In other words: Why had modern civilization to be built up laboriously as something new on the ruins of the old, instead of being a direct continuation of it?

F. W. Walbank
THE NATURE OF THE PROBLEM

Frank William Walbank, Rathbone Professor of Ancient History and Classical Archaeology in the University of Liverpool, was born in 1909 and educated at Cambridge. He is the author of biographies of Aratus of Sicyon and Philip V of Macedon. Volumes I and II of his major work, A Historical Commentary on Polybius, *were published in 1957 and 1967.*

[*After briefly summarizing the views of the decline of the Roman Empire held by such men as Petrarch, Machiavelli, Voltaire, and Gibbon, the author continues:*]

These examples may serve to illustrate the peculiarly topical shape which the problem of the decline of Rome invariably assumed. From it each age in turn has tried to formulate its own conception of progress and decadence. What, men have asked repeatedly, is the criterion by which we determine the point at which a society begins to decay? What is the yardstick by which we are to measure progress? And what are the symptoms and causes of decadence? The variety of answers given to these questions is calculated to depress the inquiring reader. When so many representative thinkers can find so many and such various explanations, according to the age in which they live, is there any hope, he will ask, of an answer that can claim more than purely relative validity?

The problem of progress and decadence (if we may so term it) has indeed evoked a variety of solutions. At some periods, as we have seen—particularly during the Renaissance—the question is broached in terms of political issues; society goes forward or back according to how it settles questions of popular liberty, the power of the state,

Reprinted by permission of Lawrence & Wishart Ltd., from F. W. Walbank, *The Decline of the Roman Empire in the West* (New York, 1953), pp. 3–7.

the existence of tensions within its own structure. At other times the moral note is struck: decay appears as a decline in ethical standards, whether through the removal of salutary threats from without or through the incursion of luxury. Both these approaches are essentially "naturalistic" in that they attempt to deduce the forms of progress and decadence from man's own acts, moral or political; and they stand in contrast to what has, on the whole, been the more usual attitude to the problem—the religious or mystical approach.

By some the rise and fall of empires have been interpreted (as among the early Christians) in prophetic terms, so as to conform with an apocalyptic picture of "four world kingdoms" or "six world ages." Another view treats history as a succession of civilizations, each reproducing the growth and decline of a living organism, in accordance with a kind of biological law. Or again civilizations are regarded as developing in cycles, one following straight after and repeating another, so that history is virtually a revolving wheel. Propounded originally by Plato (c. 427–347 B.C.) this cyclical theory found favor with Polybius (c. 200–117 B.C.), the Greek historian of Rome's rise to power, who thought it explained certain signs of decadence which his keen eye had detected at the height of Roman success. Taken over from Polybius by Machiavelli, this cyclical theory was adapted by G. B. Vico in the eighteenth century, and has its disciples in our own day. Similarly, the biological conception has become part of the common currency of historical writing. "The vast fabric," a modern scholar and statesman has written of the Roman Empire,[1] "succumbed in time, as all human institutions do, to the law of decay." All generalizations of this kind are at the root mystical.

These various answers seem largely to depend on where one starts. And perhaps the most satisfactory starting-point is the body which itself progresses and decays. For progress and decay are functions, not of isolated individuals, but of men and women knit together in society. It is society which goes forward or backward; and civilization is essentially a quality of social man. Aristotle made this point when he defined the state as originating in the bare needs of life and continuing in existence for the sake of the good life (*Politics* I.2.8, 1252*b*). Evidently, therefore, when we say a society is in decay, we refer to something having gone wrong within its structure, or in

[1] H. H. Asquith, *The Legacy of Rome,* ed. Cyril Bailey (Oxford, 1923), p. 1.

the relationship between the various groups which compose it. The problem of decadence, like the problem of progress, is at the root a problem of man in society.

Now it is precisely this fact which gives ground for hoping that today it may be possible to say something new, and something of absolute validity upon the problem of the decline of the Roman Empire. For it is in our knowledge of the social man of antiquity that there has been the greatest revolution in the classical studies of the last sixty years.

In the past, ancient history was inevitably subjected to a double distortion. Our knowledge of the past could come in the main only from the writers of the past. In the last resort historians were dependent on their literary sources, and had to accept, roughly speaking, the world these drew. In addition there was the bias which the historian himself invariably imports into what he writes, rendered the more dangerous because he could let his fancy play, with no external control beyond his literary sources. Today the picture is quite different. For over fifty years classical scholars of many nationalities have been busy digging, classifying and interpreting material which was never meant for the historian's eye, and is for that reason invaluable evidence about the age which produced it. Buried towns like Pompeii and Herculaneum, with their houses, shops and equipment; inscriptions set up to embody some government decree in Athens or Ephesus, or to record some financial transaction on Delos, or the manumission of a slave at Delphi; the dedication of countless soldiers to their favorite deity, Mithras or perhaps some purely local goddess, like Coventina at Carrawburgh in Northumberland; papyrus fragments of household accounts and the libraries of great houses, salvaged from the sand of Oxyrhyncus and the mummy-cases of Roman Egypt; together with a scientific rereading and reinterpreting of the ancient texts in the light of this new knowledge, all these have opened up new vistas for the historian of social and economic life.

Now for the first time it is possible to turn a microscope on the ancient world. From the consideration of thousands of separate instances, general trends have been deduced, statistical laws have been established. We can now see beyond the individual to the life of society as a whole; and with that change in perspective we are able to determine directions where the literary sources showed us none. This does not, of course, mean that the classical authors may now be neglected. On the contrary they have become doubly valuable, for the light they throw on (and receive from) the new evidence. For consecutive history we still depend on the literary sources with their personal details; but the new discoveries give them a new dimension, particularly in all that concerns social or "statistical" man. The bias of our sources has thus largely been overcome; and though the presuppositions of the historian himself survive as an indissoluble residuum, the scientific, "indisputable" character of the new evidence frequently controls the answer, like the materials of a laboratory experiment. Thus for the first time in history it has become possible to analyze the course of decay in the Roman world with a high degree of objectivity.

A. H. M. Jones
EAST AND WEST

Arnold Hugh Martin Jones was born in 1904 and died in 1970. He was educated at Oxford where he later held a lectureship. Subsequently he held the position of Professor of Ancient History at University College, London and at Cambridge University. The author of many works on ancient Greek as well as Roman history, his main interest was in economic and social history and in the history of institutions. The excerpts in this volume represent the conclusions he reached after a lifetime of consideration of Roman imperial history.

The sack of Rome by Alaric in 410 caused a tremendous shock to Christians and pagans alike. Jerome, when he heard the news in Bethlehem, declared: "When the brightest light on the whole earth was extinguished, when the Roman empire was deprived of its head, when, to speak more correctly, the whole world perished in one city, then 'I was dumb with silence. I held my peace, even from good, and my sorrow was stirred.'" Only a decade earlier Claudian had written: "There will never be an end to the power of Rome," and Ammianus

Reprinted by permission of the publisher from A. H. M. Jones, *The Later Roman Empire, 284–602 A.D.* (3 vols.; Oxford: Basil Blackwell, 1964), Vol. 2, pp. 1025–27.

had believed that "as long as there are men Rome will be victorious and will increase with lofty growth." The fall of Rome spelled the fall of the empire; it even meant the end of the world. A century before Lactantius had written: "The fall and ruin of the world will soon take place, but it seems that nothing of the kind is to be feared as long as the city of Rome stands intact. But when the capital of the world has fallen . . . who can doubt that the end will have come for the affairs of men and for the whole world? It is that city which sustains all things."

To pagans the explanation of the catastrophe was only too obvious. The misfortunes of the empire had increased with the growth of Christianity. The final disaster had come only a few years after Theodosius the Great had closed the temples and banned the worship of the gods. It was plain that the ancient gods by whose favor Rome had climbed to universal power had withdrawn their protection and were chastising the faithless Romans who had abandoned their worship.

The Christians made several answers, none of them very convincing. Orosius in his *Historia contra Paganos* set out to prove that the history of Rome while she still worshipped the gods had been one uninterrupted series of disasters, and that with the barbarians in Spain and Gaul exterminating one another and vying to take service under the empire, things were now at last taking a turn for the better. This was too perverse to carry conviction to any reasonable man. Despite occasional misfortunes Rome had been victorious and had won a great empire under the old dispensation. Things did not get better, but went from bad to worse, and Salvian a generation later took a quite different line in his *de Gubernatione Dei.* The disasters of the empire, he argued, were the chastisement inflicted by God on the Romans for their sins, their loose sexual morals, their oppression of the poor, and their addiction to the games. By contrast, reviving the legend of the noble savage, he pictured the barbarians as perhaps uncouth but chaste, austere and righteous. The refugees whose homes had been plundered and burned, the free men who had been carried off and sold into slavery, the sacred virgins whom the Vandals had raped by the score, cannot have found Salvian's arguments very convincing.

Augustine in *The City of God* used both these arguments, but his main theme was different. It was true, he admitted, that in the *civitas terrena* pagan Rome had prospered and the history of the Christian empire had been calamitous. But what did the things of this world matter in comparison with the spiritual world, the *civitas Dei*? To the Christian earthly disasters were indifferent, they were even to be welcomed as sent by God to discipline and purify the faithful. This world was only a vale of tears, and true blessedness was to be found in the life of the spirit here on earth, and in all its fullness in the world to come.

In the eighteenth century the debate on the fall of the empire was resumed, and it has gone on ever since. Rationalists like Gibbon saw religion as a primary cause of its decline, but in a very different way from the pagan and Christian controversialists of the fifth century. Christianity in his view sapped the morale of the empire, deadened its intellectual life and by its embittered controversies undermined its unity. Other historians, according to the temper of their times, have emphasized the empire's military decline, its political or social weaknesses, or its economic decay.

All the historians who have discussed the decline and fall of the Roman Empire have been Westerners. Their eyes have been fixed on the collapse of Roman authority in the Western parts and the evolution of the medieval Western European world. They have tended to forget, or to brush aside, one very important fact, that the Roman Empire, though it may have declined, did not fall in the fifth century nor indeed for another thousand years. During the fifth century, while the Western parts were being parceled out into a group of barbarian kingdoms, the empire of the East stood its ground. In the sixth it counterattacked and reconquered Africa from the Vandals and Italy from the Ostrogoths, and part of Spain from the Visigoths. Before the end of the century, it is true, much of Italy and Spain had succumbed to renewed barbarian attacks, and in the seventh the onslaught of the Arabs robbed the empire of Syria, Egypt, and Africa, and the Slavs overran the Balkans. But in Asia Minor the empire lived on, and later, recovering its strength, reconquered much territory that it had lost in the dark days of the seventh century.

These facts are important, for they demonstrate that the empire did not, as some modern historians have suggested, totter into its grave from senile decay, impelled by a gentle push from the barbarians. Most of the internal weaknesses which these historians stress were common to both halves of the empire. The East was even more

Christian than the West, its theological disputes far more embittered. The East, like the West, was administered by a corrupt and extortionate bureaucracy. The Eastern government strove as hard to enforce a rigid caste system, tying the *curiales* to their cities and the *coloni* to the soil. Land fell out of cultivation and was deserted in the East as well as in the West. It may be that some of these weaknesses were more accentuated in the West than in the East, but this is a question which needs investigation. It may be also that the initial strength of the Eastern empire in wealth and population was greater, and that it could afford more wastage; but this again must be demonstrated.

II THE CAUSES

J. B. Bury
DECLINE AND CALAMITIES OF THE EMPIRE

John Bagnell Bury was born in Dublin in 1861 and was educated there at Trinity College. From 1902 until his death in 1927 he was Regius Professor of Modern History at Cambridge University. His textbook on the history of Greece remains a classic in its field, as does his Ancient Greek Historians. *His edition of Gibbon is the best ever done. Bury's interest in the philosophy of history is demonstrated by two of his works,* The History of Freedom of Thought *and* The Idea of Progress.

The explanations of the calamities of the Empire which have been hazarded by modern writers are of a different order from those which occurred to witnesses of the events, but they are not much more satisfying. The illustrious historian whose name will always be associated with the "Decline" of the Roman Empire invoked "the principle of decay," a principle which has itself to be explained. Depopulation, the Christian religion, the fiscal system have all been assigned as causes of the Empire's decline in strength. If these or any of them were responsible for its dismemberment by the barbarians in the West, it may be asked how it was that in the East, where the same causes operated, the Empire survived much longer intact and united.

Consider depopulation. The depopulation of Italy was an important fact and it had far-reaching consequences. But it was a process which had probably reached its limit in the time of Augustus. There is no evidence that the Empire was less populous in the fourth and fifth centuries than in the first. The "sterility of the human harvest" in Italy and Greece affected the history of the Empire from its very beginning, but does not explain the collapse in the fifth century. The truth is that there are two distinct questions which have been confused. It is one thing to seek the causes which changed the Roman state from what it was in the best days of the Republic to what it had become in the age of Theodosius the Great—a change which from certain points of view may be called a "decline." It is quite another thing to ask why the state which could resist its enemies on many frontiers in

From J. B. Bury, *History of the Later Roman Empire, 395–565* (2 vols.; London, 1923), Vol. I, 308–13. Reprinted by permission of Macmillan & Company Ltd. (London).

the days of Diocletian and Constantine and Julian suddenly gave way
in the days of Honorius. "Depopulation" may partly supply the answer to the first question, but it is not an answer to the second. Nor
can the events which transferred the greater part of western Europe
to German masters be accounted for by the numbers of the peoples
who invaded it. The notion of vast hosts of warriors, numbered by
hundreds of thousands, pouring over the frontiers, is, as we saw,
perfectly untrue. The total number of one of the large East German
nations probably seldom exceeded 100,000, and its army of fighting
men can rarely have been more than from 20,000 to 30,000. They
were not a deluge, overwhelming and irresistible, and the Empire had
a well-organized military establishment at the end of the fourth century, fully sufficient in capable hands to beat them back. As a matter
of fact, since the defeat at Hadrianople which was due to the blun-
ders of Valens, no very important battle was won by German over
Imperial forces during the whole course of the invasions.

It has often been alleged that Christianity in its political effects
was a disintegrating force and tended to weaken the power of Rome
to resist her enemies. It is difficult to see that it had any such
tendency, so long as the Church itself was united. Theological
heresies were indeed to prove a disintegrating force in the East in
the seventh century, when differences in doctrine which had alienated the Christians in Egypt and Syria from the government of Constantinople facilitated the conquests of the Saracens. But, after the
defeat of Arianism, there was no such vital or deep-reaching division
in the West, and the effect of Christianity was to unite, not to sever,
to check, rather than to emphasize, national or sectional feeling. In
the political calculations of Constantine it was probably this idea of
unity, as a counterpoise to the centrifugal tendencies which had
been clearly revealed in the third century, that was the great recom-
mendation of the religion which he raised to power. Nor is there the
least reason to suppose that Christian teaching had the practical
effect of making men less loyal to the Empire or less ready to defend
it. The Christians were as pugnacious as the pagans. Some might
read Augustine's *City of God* with edification, but probably very few
interpreted its theory with such strict practical logic as to be indifferent to the safety of the Empire. Hardly the author himself, though this
has been disputed.

It was not long after Alaric's capture of Rome that Volusian, a pagan senator of a distinguished family, whose mother was a Christian and a friend of Augustine, proposed the question whether the teaching of Christianity is not fatal to the welfare of a state, because a Christian smitten on one cheek would if he followed the precepts of the Gospel turn the other to the smiter. We have the letter in which Augustine answers the question and skillfully explains the text so as to render it consistent with common sense. And to show that warfare is not forbidden, another text is quoted in which soldiers who ask "What shall we do?" are bidden to "Do violence to no man, neither accuse any falsely, and be content with your wages." They are not told not to serve or fight. The bishop goes on to suggest that those who wage a just war are really acting *misericorditer,* in a spirit of mercy and kindness to their enemies, as it is to the true interests of their enemies that their vices should be corrected. Augustine's *misericorditer* laid down unintentionally a dangerous and hypocritical doctrine for the justification of war, the same principle which was used for justifying the Inquisition. But his definite statement that the Christian discipline does not condemn all wars was equivalent to saying that Christians were bound as much as pagans to defend Rome against the barbarians. And this was the general view. All the leading Churchmen of the fifth century were devoted to the Imperial idea, and when they worked for peace or compromise, as they often did, it was always when the cause of the barbarians was in the ascendant and resistance seemed hopeless.

The truth is that the success of the barbarians in penetrating and founding states in the western provinces cannot be explained by any general considerations. It is accounted for by the actual events and would be clearer if the story were known more fully. The gradual collapse of the Roman power in this section of the Empire was the consequence of *a series of contingent events.* No general causes can be assigned that made it inevitable.

The first contingency was the irruption of the Huns into Europe, an event resulting from causes which were quite independent of the weakness or strength of the Roman Empire. It drove the Visigoths into the Illyrian provinces, and the difficult situation was unhappily mismanaged. One Emperor was defeated and lost his life; it was his own fault. That disaster, which need not have occurred, was a second contingency. His successor allowed a whole federate nation to settle on provincial soil; he took the line of least resistance and

established an unfortunate precedent. He did not foresee consequences which, if he had lived ten or twenty years longer, might not
have ensued. His death was a third contingency. But the situation
need have given no reason for grave alarm if the succession had
passed to an Emperor like himself, or Valentinian I, or even Gratian.
Such a man was not procreated by Theodosius and the government
of the West was inherited by a feeble-minded boy. That was a fourth
event, dependent on causes which had nothing to do with the condition of the Empire.

In themselves these events need not have led to disaster. If the
guardian of Honorius and director of his government had been a man
of Roman birth and tradition, who commanded the public confidence, a man such as Honorius himself was afterwards to find in
Constantius and his successor in Aetius, all might have been tolera-
bly well, But there was a point of weakness in the Imperial system,
the practice of elevating Germans to the highest posts of command
in the army. It had grown up under Valentinian I, Gratian, and
Theodosius; it had led to the rebellion of Maximus, and had cost
Valentinian II his life. The German in whom Theodosius reposed his
confidence and who assumed the control of affairs on his death
probably believed that he was serving Rome faithfully, but it was a
singular misfortune that at a critical moment when the Empire had to
be defended not only against Germans without but against a German
nation which had penetrated inside, the responsibility should have
devolved upon a German. Stilicho did not intend to be a traitor, but
his policy was as calamitous as if he had planned deliberate
treachery. For it meant civil war. The dissatisfaction of the Romans in
the West was expressed in the rebellion of Constantine, the successor of Maximus, and if Stilicho had had his way the soldiers of
Honorius and of Arcadius would have been killing one another for
the possession of Illyricum. When he died the mischief was done;
Goths had Italy at their mercy, Gaul and Spain were overrun by other
peoples. His Roman successors could not undo the results of events
which need never have happened.

The supremacy of a Stilicho was due to the fact that the defense
of the Empire had come to depend on the enrollment of barbarians,
in large numbers, in the army, and that it was necessary to render the
service attractive to them by the prospect of power and wealth. This
was, of course, a consequence of the decline in military spirit, and of

depopulation, in the old civilized Mediterranean countries. The Germans in high command had been useful, but the dangers involved in the policy had been shown in the cases of Merobaudes and Arbogastes. Yet this policy need not have led to the dismemberment of the Empire, and but for that series of chances its western provinces would not have been converted, as and when they were, into German kingdoms. It may be said that a German penetration of western Europe must ultimately have come about. But even if that were certain, it might have happened in another way, at a later time, more gradually, and with less violence. The point of the present contention is that Rome's loss of her provinces in the fifth century was not an "inevitable effect of any of those features which have been rightly or wrongly described as causes or consequences of her general 'decline.' " The central fact that Rome could not dispense with the help of barbarians for her wars *(gentium barbararum auxilio indigemus)* may be held to be the cause of her calamities, but it was a weakness which might have continued to be far short of fatal but for the sequence of contingencies pointed out above.

Edward Gibbon

GENERAL OBSERVATIONS ON THE FALL OF THE ROMAN EMPIRE IN THE WEST

Edward Gibbon was born in Putney, England in 1737. His great work, Decline and Fall of the Roman Empire, *published between 1776 and 1788, brought him fame and membership in the illustrious circle of Dr. Johnson. It is one of the great classics of historical literature and one of the best products of the thought of the eighteenth-century Enlightenment.*

The Greeks, after their country had been reduced into a province, imputed the triumphs of Rome, not to the merit, but to the *Fortune* of the republic. The inconstant goddess, who so blindly distributes and resumes her favors, had *now* consented (such was the language of

From Edward Gibbon, *Decline and Fall of the Roman Empire* (London, 1901), Vol. IV, pp. 160–63.

envious flattery) to resign her wings, to descend from her globe, and to fix her firm and immutable throne on the banks of the Tiber. A wiser Greek, who has composed, with a philosophic spirit, the memorable history of his own times, deprived his countrymen of this vain and delusive comfort by opening to their view the deep foundations of the greatness of Rome. The fidelity of the citizens to each other, and to the state, was confirmed by the habits of education and the prejudices of religion. Honor, as well as virtue, was the principle of the republic; the ambitious citizens labored to deserve the solemn glories of a triumph; and the ardor of the Roman youth was kindled into active emulation, as often as they beheld the domestic images of their ancestors. The temperate struggles of the patricians and plebeians had finally established the firm and equal balance of the constitution; which united the freedom of popular assemblies with the authority and wisdom of a senate and the executive powers of a regal magistrate. When the consul displayed the standard of the republic, each citizen bound himself, by the obligation of an oath, to draw his sword in the cause of his country, till he had discharged the sacred duty by a military service of ten years. This wise institution continually poured into the field the rising generations of freemen and soldiers; and their numbers were reinforced by the warlike and populous states of Italy, who, after a brave resistance, had yielded to the valor, and embraced the alliance, of the Romans. The sage historian, who excited the virtue of the younger Scipio and beheld the ruin of Carthage, has accurately described their military system; their levies, arms, exercises, subordination, marches, encampments; and the invincible legion, superior in active strength to the Macedonian phalanx of Philip and Alexander. From these institutions of peace and war, Polybius has deduced the spirit and success of a people incapable of fear and impatient of repose. The ambitious design of conquest, which might have been defeated by the seasonable conspiracy of mankind, was attempted and achieved; and the perpetual violation of justice was maintained by the political virtues of prudence and courage. The arms of the republic, sometimes vanquished in battle, always victorious in war, advanced with rapid steps to the Euphrates, the Danube, the Rhine, and the Ocean; and the images of gold, or silver, or brass, that might serve to represent the nations and their kings, were successively broken by the *iron* monarchy of Rome.

The rise of a city, which swelled into an empire, may deserve, as a singular prodigy, the reflection of a philosophic mind. But the decline of Rome was the natural and inevitable effect of immoderate greatness. Prosperity ripened the principle of decay; the causes of destruction multiplied with the extent of conquest; and, as soon as time or accident had removed the artificial supports, the stupendous fabric yielded to the pressure of its own weight. The story of its ruin is simple and obvious; and, instead of inquiring why the Roman empire was destroyed, we should rather be surprised that it had subsisted so long. The victorious legions, who, in distant wars, acquired the vices of strangers and mercenaries, first oppressed the freedom of the republic, and afterwards violated the majesty of the purple. The emperors, anxious for their personal safety and the public peace, were reduced to the base expedient of corrupting the discipline which rendered them alike formidable to their sovereign and to the enemy; the vigor of the military government was relaxed, and finally dissolved, by the partial institutions of Constantine; and the Roman world was overwhelmed by a deluge of Barbarians.

The decay of Rome has been frequently ascribed to the translation of the seat of empire; but this history has already shown that the powers of government were *divided* rather than *removed*. The throne of Constantinople was erected in the East; while the West was still possessed by a series of emperors who held their residence in Italy and claimed their equal inheritance of the legions and provinces. This dangerous novelty impaired the strength, and fomented the vices, of a double reign; the instruments of an oppressive and arbitrary system were multiplied; and a vain emulation of luxury, not of merit, was introduced and supported between the degenerate successors of Theodosius. Extreme distress, which unites the virtue of a free people, embitters the factions of a declining monarchy. The hostile favorites of Arcadius and Honorius betrayed the republic to its common enemies; and the Byzantine court beheld with indifference, perhaps with pleasure, the disgrace of Rome, the misfortunes of Italy, and the loss of the West. Under the succeeding reigns, the alliance of the two empires was restored; but the aid of the Oriental Romans was tardy, doubtful, and ineffectual; and the national schism of the Greeks and Latins was enlarged by the perpetual difference of language and manners, of interest, and even of religion. Yet the salutary event approved in some measure the judgment of Constantine. During a long period of decay, his impregnable city repelled the victorious armies of Barbarians, protected the wealth of Asia, and commanded, both in peace and war, the important straits which connect the Euxine and Mediterranean seas. The foundation of Constantinople more essentially contributed to the preservation of the East than to the ruin of the West.

As the happiness of a *future* life is the great object of religion, we may hear, without surprise or scandal, that the introduction, or at least the abuse, of Christianity had some influence on the decline and fall of the Roman Empire. The clergy successfully preached the doctrines of patience and pusillanimity; the active virtues of society were discouraged; and the last remains of the military spirit were buried in the cloister; a large portion of public and private wealth was consecrated to the specious demands of charity and devotion; and the soldiers' pay was lavished on the useless multitudes of both sexes, who could only plead the merits of abstinence and chastity. Faith, zeal, curiosity, and the more earthly passions of malice and ambition kindled the flame of theological discord; the church, and even the state, were distracted by religious factions, whose conflicts were sometimes bloody, and always implacable; the attention of the emperors was diverted from camps to synods; the Roman world was oppressed by a new species of tyranny; and the persecuted sects became the secret enemies of their country. Yet party spirit, however pernicious or absurd, is a principle of union as well as of dissension. The bishops, from eighteen hundred pulpits, inculcated the duty of passive obedience to a lawful and orthodox sovereign; their frequent assemblies, and perpetual correspondence, maintained the communion of distant churches; and the benevolent temper of the gospel was strengthened, though confined, by the spiritual alliance of the Catholics. The sacred indolence of the monks was devoutly embraced by a servile and effeminate age; but, if superstition had not afforded a decent retreat, the same vices would have tempted the unworthy Romans to desert, from baser motives, the standard of the republic. Religious precepts are easily obeyed, which indulge and sanctify the natural inclinations of their votaries; but the pure and genuine influence of Christianity may be traced in its beneficial, though imperfect, effects on the Barbarian proselytes of the North. If the decline of the Roman Empire was hastened by the conversion of Constantine, his victorious religion broke the violence of the fall, and mollified the ferocious temper of the conquerors.

F. W. Walbank

TRENDS IN THE EMPIRE OF THE SECOND CENTURY A.D.

I

The *pax Augusta* brought prosperity to a wide area of the earth's surface; but it completely failed to release new productive forces. As in the century after Alexander's death in 323 B.C.—a century in many ways comparable to the early Empire—the step to industrialization and the factory was never taken. Indeed, except for a few new devices like the mill-wheel, the level of technique inside the Roman Empire never surpassed that already reached at Alexandria. Nor was this due to any special Roman foible; on the contrary it continued the classical tradition of the Alexandrines, who could find no better use for many of their mechanical devices than to impress the ignorant congregations in the Egyptian temples and to bolster up their religion with sham miracles. For the origins of this tradition one must go back to the Greek city-state.

From its outset classical civilization inherited a low level of technical skill, judged by the part Greece and Rome were destined to play in history. The Greek tribes settled in a poor and rocky land; only by incessant labor could Hesiod wring a livelihood from the soil of Boeotia. Consequently, the leisure which was to bring forth the Ionian Renaissance and the fine flower of Periclean Athens could only be purchased at a price. The temples on the Acropolis, the plays in the theater of Dionysus, the speculations of Plato, were only possible because an army of women, resident foreigners, slaves and imperial subjects supported by their toil a leisured minority of full citizens. The position at Rome was similar. There the wealth of the late republic was built up . . . on the sweat of the provinces, the loot of many wars, and the sufferings of countless slaves enduring abject misery on the plantations of aristocratic landowners, resident in Rome. This relationship of absentee landlord and plantation slave reproduced in an accentuated form that contrast which underlay ancient civilization, between the leisured class of the city and the multitude laboring to

Reprinted by permission of Lawrence and Wishart Ltd., from F. W. Walbank, *The Decline of the Roman Empire in the West* (New York, 1953), pp. 21–37, 67–69.

support it on the land—a contrast which evoked a famous criticism of the cities of the Empire as "hives of drones."

This antithesis was no new thing; like the low level of classical technique, it had been characteristic of the ancient civilizations which sprang up in the river valleys of Egypt, Mesopotamia and the Punjab round about the third millennium B.C. Common to the east too was the institution of slavery, which spread from the home to the mine and the plantation, to become the basis of Greek and Roman civilization, a cancer in the flesh of society which grew with society itself. Slavery was never effectively challenged. Aristotle (384–322 B.C.), one of the most acute philosophers and students of political science who ever lived, laid it down as axiomatic that "from the hour of their birth some are marked out for subjection, others for rule" (*Politics,* I.5.2, 1254a); "the art of war" he wrote "is a natural art of acquisition, for it includes hunting, an art which we ought to practice against wild beasts and against men who, though intended by nature to be governed, will not submit; for war of such a kind is naturally just" (*Politics,* I.8.12, 1256b). It is perhaps not strange that a philosopher who so faithfully reflects the practice of his own society in framing his definition of a just war should also have sought to demonstrate the natural inferiority of woman to man.

After Aristotle another school of philosophers arose, the Stoics, who for a short time asserted the equality of slaves and free men; but they never passed from this to the obvious conclusion that slavery should be abolished. Very soon they too lapsed back into the easier Aristotelian view. Meanwhile slavery was spreading both geographically and in the number of human beings which it enveloped in its folds. The wars of Alexander's successors and of the Roman republic brought a constantly increasing supply; especially on the plantations and sheep ranches and in the mines they formed an indispensable source of labor. At Rome "Sardinians for sale" became a proverb for anything in cheap supply; and Strabo has left us a picture of the famous slave-market of Delos in the late second century B.C. (XIV, 668); "the island," he writes "could admit and send away tens of thousands of slaves in the same day. . . . The cause of this was the fact that the Romans, having become rich after the destruction of Carthage and Corinth (146 B.C.), used many slaves; and the pirates, seeing the easy profit therein, bloomed forth in great numbers, themselves not only going in quest of booty, but also trafficking in slaves."

It was this slavery at the root of society which controlled the general pattern of classical civilization. For it split up every community into two kinds of human beings—the free man and the slave; and it ordained that those who did the basic work of society should not be those to benefit from it. The natural outcome was that the slave lacked the incentive to master and improve the technique of the work he was doing. Equally disastrous was the effect upon the slave-owners themselves. Because it became normal to associate manual labor with slaves, Greek culture began to draw a line between the things of the hand and the things of the mind. In the *Republic,* Plato (*c.* 429–347 B.C.) pictured a utopian community divided into three sharply differentiated classes, endowed each with some imaginary "metallic" quality—Guardians with a golden cast of mind, to govern; Auxiliaries with an admixture of silver, to fight and police the state; and finally Workers, sharing in the base metals, to do the work of society and to obey. Aristotle, with an equal contempt for manual work, writes: "Doubtless in ancient times the artisan class were slaves or foreigners, and therefore the majority of them are so now. The best form of state will not admit them to citizenship" (*Politics,* III.5.3, 1278*a*). "Certainly the good man . . . and the good citizen ought not to learn the crafts of inferiors except for their own occasional use; if they habitually practice these, there will cease to be a distinction between master and slave" (*Politics,* III.4.13, 1277*b*).

The Roman attitude varied no whit from this. Cicero's formulation deserves to be quoted in full. "Public opinion," he writes (*De Officiis,* I, 150–51),

divides the trades and professions into the liberal and the vulgar. We condemn the odious occupation of the collector of customs and the usurer, and the base and menial work of unskilled laborers; for the very wages the laborer receives are a badge of slavery. Equally contemptible is the business of the retail dealer; for he cannot succeed unless he is dishonest, and dishonesty is the most shameful thing in the world. The work of the mechanic is also degrading; there is nothing noble about a workshop. The least respectable of all trades are those which minister to pleasure, as Terence tells us, "fishmongers, butchers, cooks, sausage-makers." Add to these if you like, perfumers, dancers, and the actors of the gaming-house. But the learned professions, such as medicine, ar-

chitecture and the higher education, from which society derives the
greatest benefit, are considered honorable occupations for those to
whose social position they are appropriate. Business on a small scale is
despicable; but if it is extensive and imports commodities in large quantities from all over the world and distributes them honestly, it is not so
very discreditable; nay, if the merchant, satiated, or rather satisfied, with
the fortune he has made, retires from the harbor and steps into an estate,
as once he returned to harbor from the sea, he deserves, I think, the
highest respect. But of all the sources of wealth farming is the best, the
most able, the most profitable, the most noble.*

Government at Rome throughout the period of the republic was in
the hands of an aristocratic clique whose wealth was derived from
land and which had debarred itself from commerce by a self-denying
ordinance. This caste was the natural opponent of any economic
improvement which challenged its own position. After the conquest
of Macedonia in 168 B.C. it closed down the Macedonian mines lest
they should strengthen the commercial elements which would have
worked them; and once current needs could be met from the
Spanish mines, the Senate practically stopped mining in Italy. "This
maintained Senatorial authority beyond challenge: but it also
checked the economic expansion which might have restored the
balance in the country."

It was this landed class which peopled the countryside of Italy and
Sicily with the slave gangs which later threatened Rome's very existence in the revolt of Spartacus (73–71 B.C.). Meanwhile the towns
and cities were filling up with eastern slaves, who not only undertook
all kinds of manual work, but also acted as teachers, doctors, architects and professional men. The consequence was that socially
these activities were ill thought of. "The meaner sort of mechanic has
a special and separate slavery," wrote Aristotle (*Politics*, I.13.13,
1260a); and similarly the Romans despised the free artisan as one
doing work proper to a slave. Thus the atmosphere was wholly unfavorable to technical progress in a field for which anyone of any
consequence had nothing but contempt. When labor is cheap and
worthless, why conserve it? So the classical world perpetuated that
technical retardation which had been one of the most paradoxical
features of the civilizations of the Nile and Euphrates—paradoxical
because it was thanks to a unique crop of technical inventions—the
plow, the wheeled cart, the sailing boat, the solar calendar, the
smelting of copper ores, the use of the power of oxen and the

harnessing of the winds with sails—that these civilizations had come into being. In both instances the cause of retardation was the same—the bisection of society into classes with contrary interests.

Economically, this division of society ensured that the vast masses of the Empire never tasted the fruits of their labor; and this meant a permanently restricted internal market. Because wealth was concentrated at the top, the body of society suffered from chronic underconsumption. Accordingly industry had to seek its market either in the limited circle of the middle and upper class, together with the army (which therefore had considerable economic significance), or else outside the Empire, where of course there were even fewer markets for mass-produced goods. Consequently, the economic basis for industrialization was not to hand. The expansion of the Empire brought new markets, which staved off the problem for a time; but, as we shall see, the effects of this expansion were soon cancelled out by the decentralization of production and were never radical enough to carry a large-scale industry, using all the resources of advanced technique and advanced forms of power.

On the other hand, because of the social structure, Greece and Rome never even considered the possibility of catering for the proletariat and peasantry, and so creating a deeper, instead of a wider, market. What expansion the Empire brought proves on closer examination to be "a matter of greater extension, not of greater depth." The *pax Augusta* removed many handicaps and much wastage; goods circulated with greater ease and over wider areas. But there was no qualitative change in the nature of classical economy. In one field alone were there notable technical achievements—in that of building and engineering, where the Hellenistic Age had already given a lead, under the stimulus of interstate warfare; but even here the Romans were concerned with the amplifying and application of old processes rather than with the creation of new. Thus behind the rosy hues of Gibbon's picture of a prosperous Antonine world we are now in a position to detect at least one fatal weakness—the complete stagnation of technique.

II

It has been suggested above that in the long run the expansion of the Roman Empire could bring only a temporary fillip to its economy.

The reason why this was so deserves special attention, for it illumi-
nates a factor of some importance for our central problem. Modern
investigation has revealed in the Roman Empire the operation of an
economic law which finds its application equally in our own
society—the centrifugal tendency of industry to export itself instead
of its products, and of trades to migrate from the older areas of the
economy to the new.

The operation of this law has been felt with full force in this
country, since India began to satisfy its own needs with cotton man-
ufactured in Bombay; here the lesson has been underlined by mass
unemployment in the cotton towns of Lancashire. Today this movement to the periphery is usually connected with the establishment of
the capitalistic form of production in colonial and backward areas
and, as such areas become independent states, these states use
political methods to assert an economic independence based on
local industry. "Autarky" as a feature of the national state is a characteristic of modern times. In the Roman Empire the factors were
somewhat simpler and more primitive.

Perhaps the most important reason for moving industry as near as
possible to the new market was the weakness of ancient communications. Judged by preceding ages, Roman communications were
highly developed; but in relation to the tasks the Empire set, they
were still far too primitive. Mechanically the vehicles used on land
were very inefficient; for the ancient world never discovered the
horsecollar, but employed a form of harness which half-strangled the
beast every time it tried to drag a load along. A sea voyage was
always chancy, and overseas trade a hazardous business. Even by
the time of Augustus the task of maintaining imperial communications was beginning to weigh as an intolerable burden upon the
inhabitants of the Empire. The cost of the Imperial Post, the upkeep
of the roads, the housing of traveling officials—all these fell upon the
provincial. And in spite of police and river flotillas, brigandage had
not been wholly eliminated; the inns too were often poor and unevenly distributed. The difficulties of a voyage in the first century A.D.
are illustrated by the story of St. Paul's adventures (including a
shipwreck) on board the three vessels which were necessary to bring
him from Palestine to Rome. In short, the best transport system of
the ancient world was inadequate to cope with a relatively high
circulation of consumer's goods; and to make matters worse there is

evidence that deterioration had set in from the time of Augustus onwards.

A second factor which impelled industry outwards towards its markets was the insecurity of ancient credit. Because of the risks entailed, it was always costly to raise capital for a trading venture; interest rates were high because the risk run was personal. There was no ancient equivalent of the joint-stock company with limited liability to ensure corporate responsibility for financial ventures; and banking itself remained primitive. The Empire saw no further development of the Ptolemaic system of a central bank with branch establishments; on the contrary, in Egypt there are signs of regression to a system of independent local banks.

Furthermore, the fact that ancient industry was based on slavery also influenced the movement of decentralization. For slavery as an institution was adversely affected by the Augustan peace. The steps the emperors took to end war and piracy caused a drying-up of the main source of supply. The great days of the Delian slave market were gone forever; and, though under the more humane conditions of the early Empire the number of home-reared slaves was quite considerable, they were not sufficient to fill the gap, so that increasingly the Roman world had to fall back on the small trickle from outside the frontiers. Besides this, the growth of humanitarian sentiment . . . led to a widespread movement of slave-manumission. Yesterday's slave was tomorrow's freedman; and his grandsons would be full Roman citizens. Clearly the normal basis of ancient capitalistic activity was being undermined. And this led to a shifting of industry to more primitive lands where, as in Gaul, industry had available, if not new slaves, what was perhaps better, a free proletariat willing to turn its hands to manual labor. In the Celtic lands, as in Ptolemaic Egypt, we find free workers engaged in industrial production. Whereas in the potteries of Arretium in Italy, before A.D. 25, 123 out of 132 known workers were slaves, there is no evidence for the employment of slaves in the potteries of Gaul and the Rhine valley; and inscriptions from Dijon refer to stoneworkers and smiths as "free dependents" *(clientes)* of a local *seigneur*—an interesting sidelight on the breakup of the tribal system and the growth of social classes in Gaul. This shifting of industry contributed to the already mentioned urbanization of these backward parts; and here we may note that the new municipalities in such areas as Gaul and Spain inherited

what the Italian municipalities had largely lost—a hinterland inhabited by peasants. It has been argued that by becoming each a little
Rome in exploiting the dwellers in its own countryside the
municipalities contributed on a long-term view to their own subsequent ruin.

Another important feature of industry based on slavery was that
concentration brought no appreciable reduction of overhead expenses, as happens where power-machines are employed. Hence
there was no incentive to develop the old centers rather than expand
to new. Moreover, the simple nature of ancient equipment, the absence of complicated machinery, made it a comparatively easy business to move. Usually it would merely be a question of a few simple
tools and the skill carried in a man's own fingers. On the other hand,
the restricted internal market, which necessarily drove the merchant
farther and farther afield, combined with the constant demands of a
relatively prosperous army along the frontiers to reinforce the general
centrifugal tendency of industry. Incidentally, the army had changed
its economic role since the days of the republic. Then, as the source
of valuable plunder, it had paid its way over and over again; now, as
a peaceful garrison force, rarely fighting, and then against poor
barbarians, it was an economic liability, some 250,000 to 300,000—
rising later to 400,000 and more—idle mouths to feed—an item which
must certainly figure among the causes of Roman decline.

All these tendencies did not operate at once nor to the same
extent; but over a period of years they resulted in a clear movement
of industry outwards from the old centers of the Empire. One of the
earliest developments was that trade became local and provincial
instead of international; though, significantly, the drop in long-
distance trade in mass-produced goods did not apply to luxury articles, which still traveled virtually any distance to meet the demands
of the wealthy few. Over the whole Empire there was a gradual
reversion to small-scale, hand-to-mouth craftsmanship, producing for
the local market and for specific orders in the vicinity. Often the
movement of decentralization had two stages. Thus the manufacture
of *terra sigillata,* the universal red-ware pottery of the early Empire,
shifted first from Italy to Graufesenque in the Cevennes and thence,
in the course of the second century A.D., to Lezoux in the Allier basin,
to eastern Gaul, Rhaetia and Alsace, and finally to Rheinzabern near
Speyer. "In the African lamp industry Italian wares gave place to

Carthaginian, which themselves lost the market to lamps of purely local manufacture.''

The progress made by the various provinces was naturally uneven; sometimes the first result of decentralization was to locate some important manufacture in particularly favorable surroundings; in which case the decentralized industry might for a time capture the international market. This happened to Gallic wine and pottery, which were exported from Narbonne and Arles to the east, until the middle of the third century; pottery from Gaul is found throughout this period in Italy, Spain, Africa, Britain and even in Syria and Egypt. But on the whole this was exceptional, and in the case of Gaul and Germany was probably due to geographical factors, especially the excellent water-transport system, and also to the existence of cheap labor, conditions which were not reproduced in the older provinces of the east.

Progress in such areas as Gaul and Roman Germany was balanced by the decay of Italy. During the second century A.D. this one-time kernel of the Empire lost increasingly its predominant position. Northern Italy remained prosperous for a longer period, thanks to its links with the Danube provinces. But in the rest of the peninsula from the end of the first century A.D. onwards there appear signs of depopulation and a marked decline in the export of both agricultural and industrial products. As the trend towards decentralization developed, and as the Gallic wine-trade grew, the vineyards and olive fields of Italy shrank, making place increasingly for the cultivation of corn on large estates, farmed with serf-labor. Italy became an incubus, supported by invisible exports—officials' salaries and the Emperor's private income.

Simultaneously, at the opposite extreme, in the lands outside the frontiers, and especially to the north and northeast, among the Gauls, the Germans and the Scythians, the outward expansion of Roman trade and influence was inducing a ferment, which was to have the most far-reaching effects. Already the Gauls whom Caesar conquered (59–50 B.C.) and the Germans whom Tacitus described in his *Germania,* published in A.D. 98, had to some degree modified their earlier tribal organization; in both lands there were considerable differences of wealth, and rich counts had each their retinues of followers. But from the time of Augustus the natural development of these peoples was accelerated by the impact of Romanization. Increasingly they became involved in imperial trade currents, buying and selling across the frontiers. Increasingly they enlisted in the Roman armies as mercenaries, and on retirement took their Roman habits back to their tribes like New Guinea natives returning home from Rabaul or Sydney. Romanized chieftains employed their new culture in the service of Rome, or like Arminius, against her. In short, the centrifugal economic movement did not and could not stop at the frontiers; but overflowing into the barbarian world beyond, it carried the virtues and vices of civilization like a strong wine to unaccustomed heads. Thus it was the Romans themselves who taught the northern barbarians to look with interest and envy at the rich spoils of the Empire.

Meanwhile the process of decentralization and subdivision into smaller and smaller local economic units could have only one ultimate result—provincial autarky and the decomposition of the Empire. As one might expect, this economic tendency found its political reflection in the division of the Empire, first of all in the fourfold administration of Diocletian and his three colleagues (A.D. 286), later, after Constantine had transferred the capital to Byzantium (A.D. 330), in the permanent division into an eastern and western Empire, which laid the foundations of medieval Europe.

III

Fundamental too for medieval Europe was one particular aspect of this general movement of decentralization—the gradual transfer of industry from the cities to the villages and large country estates. In this way the essentially agrarian character of ancient civilization began to reassert itself over the urban elements which had produced its highest and most typical developments; the depressed countryside took its revenge for the long centuries during which its needs were subordinated to those of the smart men of the towns. In Italy, as we saw, vineyards and olive gardens now began to make way for large corn-growing estates; in short, intensive cultivation gave way to a less efficient and less specialized system.

Since the early days of the republic the large estate had never at any time been exceptional in the Roman world: during the Civil War of 49 B.C., Caesar records (*Bell. Civ.* I, 17) how Domitius Ahenobarbus, one of Pompey's generals, attempted to ensure his soldiers' allegiance in a tight corner by promising 1,500 men between two and three acres each out of his own private estates; and in Nero's reign, Pliny tells us (*Nat. Hist.* XVIII, 35), six men owned half the province of Africa. But then there had been countertendencies such as the granting of small allotments to retired veterans, which worked in the direction of peasant holdings. Before long these allotments ceased; and increasingly the large estate became the typical unit. Moreover it began to develop in a way which ultimately transformed its character altogether, and with it the whole system of classical economy.

In the first place, the large country estate had always been the scene of a certain amount of industry. Specially trained slaves had done the necessary farm jobs, tanning, weaving, wagon-making, fulling and work in the carpenter's or blacksmith's shop. By A.D. 50 Pliny assumes the presence of such craftsmen to be a normal feature of any estate; and by the time of Vespasian (A.D. 69–79) the emperor's own estates, organized on the pattern of the royal domains of the Hellenistic period, were setting the fashion in the provinces by becoming increasingly an agglomeration of craftsmen of every kind, as well as agricultural laborers—in fine, a self-contained community of a type common to the old Bronze Age civilizations, and later, as the manor, to medieval Christendom. Here too the regression was by no means along a straight line. Indeed, as the self-contained estate becomes increasingly a feature of the countryside of Africa, S. Russia, Italy, Asia Minor, Babylonia, Palestine and Syria, it is remarkable to watch it not simply asserting its self-sufficiency, but actually going into competition with the towns to capture the international market. With the general crisis of the third century, which hit the towns hardest, it was on such estates that economic life remained most vigorous.

The gradual drying-up of the sources of slave labor compelled the landowner to seek some other supply. Increasingly he turned to the *coloni,* not sturdy independent peasants of the old Italian type, but tenant farmers, successors of the obsolescent slave class to the doubtful privilege of being the bottom dog in the countryside. These *coloni* were usually too poor to pay rent for their land or to buy their own implements and seed; these they obtained from the landlord and, as "share-croppers," repaid him in kind and, in some provinces such as Africa, by services on his private land. Subsistence agriculture along these lines required neither traditional skill nor experience: it offered the "new rich," who arose out of the various crises of the state, an opportunity to increase their fortunes in a safe and easy fashion.

The factor of inadequate transport, already considered above, also helped the growth of these self-sufficient, "oriental," industrial estates. By making everything on the spot, the late Roman precursor of the feudal baron would eliminate the most costly item in his bill of expenses. It is not surprising that this sort of "nuclear" economy tended to attach itself to any kind of large unit engaged in primary production. It was as if industry had lost all confidence in its ability to stand alone, and must seek the prop and protection of forms of livelihood nearer to the basic needs of mankind. Not only large agricultural estates, but also mining camps, fisheries and hunting parks became to an increasing extent the nuclei around which handicrafts and industries agglomerated themselves. Sometimes these primary units were temple property, not only recalling the similar institutions of Babylon or Hellenistic Asia Minor, but also foreshadowing clearly the medieval monastery. Similarly, the new, depressed class of *coloni* were the forerunners of the later serfs.

From the time of Augustus onwards this form of "domain" economy was encroaching gradually upon the old capitalist system, based on slave labor and the free market; and it was soon followed by a catastrophic drop in every branch of agricultural technique. It is significant that after the first century A.D. agricultural literature ceased to exist as a creative force, and in its place we find the mechanical transcribing of ancient works. Yet, notwithstanding this decline in the efficiency of agricultural technique, the land continued to exercise a magnetic attraction as conditions in the towns deteriorated. . . . The State found itself obliged to make ever greater financial demands upon the bourgeoisie. From this pressure, the "nuclear" estate, worked by the methods of subsistence economy, offered its owner a safe retreat. In the late third century A.D. the Talmud directs its readers to keep a third of their estate in land, a third in cash at home, and a third invested in commerce and industry—advice which implies a recognition of the breakdown of capitalistic production and even of money economy.

This flight of industry from the towns to the manorial estates itself contributed to the general economic breakdown by reducing the effective areas open to trade. Each estate, in proportion as it became self-sufficing, meant so many more individuals subtracted from the classical economic system, so many less potential consumers for those commodities which still circulated on the old markets. So the large domain played its part in restricting trade and speeding up the general process of decentralization.

By now it must be apparent that Gibbon's picture of Rome under the Antonines needs considerable qualification. For we have traced several factors of decline rooted in the structure of Roman society, which were already beginning to operate from the time of Augustus (27 B.C.—A.D. 14), and were certainly in full swing during the period which Gibbon praised for its unique felicity. We have seen how the low level of technique in Graeco-Roman civilization had led to the development of slavery as a means of purchasing the leisure necessary for comfort and culture; and how this institution operated on both slave and master to rule out the possibility of releasing new productive forces on a scale adequate to change the material conditions of society. We have seen the restricted internal market, which followed inevitably from a social structure of this kind, bringing its own nemesis in the shape of an outward drive to seek fresh markets away from the old centers of civilization. We have seen how the backwardness of credit institutions and of communications, and the drying-up of the slave supply itself, served to reinforce this decentralizing movement, which was eventually to end in the political disintegration of the Empire. And finally we have noted the growth of the large estate, the symbol of the decline of urban civilization, and both a result of the general decay and a factor hastening it.

*   *   *

The cause of the decline of the Roman Empire is not to be sought in any one feature—in the climate, the soil, the health of the population, or indeed in any of those social and political factors which played so important a part in the actual process of decay—but rather in the whole structure of ancient society. The date at which the contradictions, which were ultimately to prove fatal, first began to appear is not A.D. 200 nor yet the setting-up of the Principate by Augustus Caesar in 27 B.C., but rather the fifth century B.C. when Athens revealed her inability to keep and broaden the middle-class democracy she had created. The failure of Athens epitomized the failure of the city-state. Built on a foundation of slave labor, or on the exploitation of similar groups, including the peasantry, the city-state yielded a brilliant minority civilization. But from the start it was topheavy. Through no fault of its citizens, but as a result of the time and place when it arose, it was supported by a woefully low level of technique. To say this is to repeat a truism. The paradoxical contrast between the spiritual achievements of Athens and her scanty material goods has long been held up to the admiration of generations who had found that a rich material inheritance did not automatically ensure richness of cultural life. But it was precisely this low level of technique, relative to the tasks Greek and Roman society set itself, that made it impossible even to consider dispensing with slavery and led to its extension from the harmless sphere of domestic labor to the mines and workshops, where it grew stronger as the contradictions of society became more apparent.

As so often, we find ourselves discussing as cause and effect factors which were constantly interacting, so that in reality the distinction between the effective agent and the result it brought about is often quite arbitrary. But roughly speaking, the city-state, precisely because it was a minority culture, tended to be aggressive and predatory, its claim to autonomy sliding over insensibly, at every opportunity, into a claim to dominate others. This led to wars, which in turn took their place among the many sources of fresh slaves. Slavery grew, and as it invaded the various branches of production it led inevitably to the damping down of scientific interest, to the cleavage, already mentioned, between the classes that used their hands and the superior class that used—and later ceased using—its mind. This ideological cleavage thus reflects a genuine separation of the community into classes; and henceforward it becomes the supreme task of even the wisest sons of the city-state—a Plato and an Aristotle—to maintain this class society, whatsoever the cost.

That cost was indeed heavy. It says much for Plato's singlemindedness that he was willing to meet it. In the *Laws,* his last attempt to plan the just city, he produces a blueprint for implanting beliefs and attitudes convenient to authority through the medium of suggestion, by a strict and ruthless censorship, the substitution of myths and emotional ceremonies for factual knowledge, the isolation of the citizen from the outside world, the creation of types with standardized reactions, and, as a final guarantee, by the sanctions of the police-state, to be invoked against all who cannot or will not conform.

Such was the intellectual and spiritual fruit of this tree, whose roots had split upon the hard rock of technical inadequacy. Materially, the result of increasing slavery was the certainty that new productive forces would not be released on any scale sufficient for a radical transformation of society. Extremes of wealth and poverty became more marked, the internal market flagged, and ancient society suffered a decline of trade and population and, finally, the wastage of class warfare. Into this sequence the rise of the Roman Empire brought the new factor of a parasitical capital; and it spread the Hellenistic system to Italy, where agrarian pauperism went side by side with imperial expansion and domination on an unparalleled scale.

From all this arose the typical developments of the social life of the Empire—industrial dispersion and a reversion to agrarian self-sufficiency—and the final attempt to retrieve the crisis, or at least to salvage whatever could be salvaged from the ruins, by the unflinching use of oppression and the machinery of the bureaucratic state. These tendencies we have already analyzed, and need not repeat them here. The important point is that they fall together into a sequence with its own logic, and that they follow—not of course in the specific details, which were determined by a thousand personal or fortuitous factors, but in their general outlines—from the premises upon which classical civilization arose, namely an absolutely low technique and, to compensate for this, the institution of slavery. Herein lie the real causes of the decline and fall of the Roman Empire.

A. E. R. Boak

MANPOWER SHORTAGE AND THE FALL OF ROME

Arthur Edward Romilly Boak was born in Halifax, Nova Scotia in 1888. For many years Professor of Ancient History at the University of Michigan, he has specialized in late Roman and Byzantine history. His History of Rome to 565 A.D. *is widely used in colleges throughout the United States.*

In this last chapter of the book [*Manpower Shortage and the Fall of the Roman Empire in the West*], I shall try to sum up the conclusions at which I arrived in the foregoing chapters and also to correlate manpower shortage with the other major factors that contributed to the collapse of the West Roman Empire in the fifth century. Let me make it clear at this point that I do not believe there was any single major cause of this collapse, but rather a combination of conditions, forces, and trends which interacted upon one another so that at times it is almost impossible to tell which was cause and which was effect. Nor do I believe it possible to indicate with any degree of exactness the point at which recessions began. Furthermore, I do not believe there was uniformity of conditions through the Western Empire as a whole, and I am quite prepared to admit that the process of decay may for a time have been arrested and, within limited areas, even temporarily reversed.

It is my conviction that I have been able to present convincing reasons, partly on the basis of contemporary evidence and partly on the strength of deductions drawn from the demographic history of other peoples, for believing that a shortage in manpower had developed within the Roman Empire as early as the last quarter of the second century. In my opinion this shortage of manpower is to be associated with, and was caused by, an actual retrogression of certain elements of the population, in particular the inhabitants of the rural areas. In this I see the explanation of such a phenomenon as the inability of the Emperor Marcus Aurelius to find the needed recruits for his army among the Romans and provincials and his

From A. E. R. Boak, *Manpower Shortage and the Fall of the Roman Empire in the West* (Ann Arbor, 1955), pp. 109–29, by permission of the University of Michigan Press.

resort to the importation of barbarians to make up the deficit. By the beginning of the third century manpower shortage was felt to be affecting the population of the towns also. Here, as an important factor may be seen the legacy of the great plague of the years 166 to 180. At any rate, Septimius Severus and others of his dynasty admitted the situation and sought to combat by legislative means some of its consequences. Their attempts to encourage agriculture and increase the rural population, their closer supervision of the occupational groups whose services appeared essential to the conduct of public business, and their impressment of the town councils as tax collecting agencies reflect both a shortage in production and a scarcity of manpower.

It has been demonstrated that by 235 the Roman Empire was showing definite symptoms of impoverishment in its human and in its material resources. I do not believe that this can be accounted for to any major extent by the effects of the war between Septimius Severus and Clodius Albinus with its resultant confiscation of the estates of the leading supporters of Severus's defeated rival. Only the proprietors and not the tillers of the soil would be affected by the change of ownership of rural estates, and the land itself would not be withdrawn from production. It is quite impossible to gauge the effects of Severus's policy upon persons engaged in commerce and industry. But the impoverishment of the urban middle class, which begins to become apparent on a wide scale in the early third century, can best be explained as a result of the impoverishment and decline of the surrounding rural population. The latter furnished the manpower to till the estates of the urban proprietors, they were the consumers of the products of local manufacture, and they were also the natural source of immigrants needed to counterbalance the normal decline in urban birth rate.

A good many years ago, in addressing a meeting of the Michigan Academy of Science, Arts, and Letters, I took occasion to emphasize the part which taxation played in the economic breakdown of the Roman Empire. I pointed out that by the third century the burden of taxation had become so heavy that it had begun to consume the capital resources of the taxpayers. This was due to the increasing costs of the imperial administration without any corresponding increase in production on the part of the population of the Empire. For this failure more than one factor was responsible. Among the causes may be mentioned the great dependence of industry upon slave labor, the lack of inventions which would stimulate production, the absence of copyright, and the unfavorable status of investors in business enterprises under Roman law. Agriculture was the main source of wealth, and production in agriculture depended upon manpower. An increase in the rural population, therefore, would have resulted in greater production, but a stationary or decreasing agrarian element would have caused stagnation or actual decline in agricultural products. As I have tried to show, there was a positive shortage of rural labor by the third century. Consequently, the increases in taxation coincided with a falling off in production and in manpower. The result was bound to be a heavier weight of taxation for the survivors and their gradual impoverishment, which, in turn, would cause a decrease in the public revenues.

It would, of course, be utterly impossible to calculate the total population loss between the death of Marcus Aurelius in 180 and that of Severus Alexander in 235. It would be just as much out of the question to try to estimate the decline in the birth rate. There were almost certainly areas where such symptoms had not yet become apparent, for example, in sections of North Africa, where the municipalities continued to expand until later in the third century. But these favorable conditions were due to special circumstances and cannot be made the basis for generalizations about Italy and the western provinces as a whole.

It has been seen how the disorders of the troubled period 235 to 284 were bound to have an extremely unfavorable effect upon the population, both rural and urban. Not only must the actual loss of life have been extremely heavy and the average longevity correspondingly reduced, but the rate of decline must have been greatly accelerated. To judge from later parallels, the population of the Roman world can hardly have recovered from the delayed effects of the epidemic of the time of Marcus Aurelius before it was struck by the equally severe and even longer pestilence of the middle third century. Also, the added losses due to war, starvation, and forcible deportation must be taken into account. Once the birth rate of a people starts to decline, it continues to do so in a geometrical and not merely an arithmetical ratio. The conclusion must therefore be reached that if even a slight decline were evident by 235, as a result of total population loss, the rate would be very noticeable by 284.

Furthermore, it would keep on becoming increasingly rapid unless or until a countertrend were established.

On the analogy of the experience of other countries, it would take a very long time even under favorable conditions for this countertrend to become effective. It is only too well known that such favorable conditions never came into being during the fourth and fifth centuries. And the evidence I have presented from the period 284–476 indicates that, in spite of the restoration of a large measure of internal peace, and notwithstanding the voluntary and involuntary immigration of barbarian peoples, the population trend was steadily downward until the end of the West Roman Empire. Herein lies the explanation of the continued decline in the population of western Europe until about 900, a phenomenon noted by students of medieval demography.

The inevitable accompaniment of the population decline was naturally a corresponding decrease in the manpower available for agriculture, industry, and the public services, a condition which became more and more acute from the late third to the fifth century. At the same time there was a corresponding decrease in agricultural and industrial production. It would be rash to say that this was due altogether to shortage of available labor since the economic policies of the Late Empire unquestionably played a considerable role in preventing a revival of prosperity. The decline in individual capital wealth was also a factor of importance. In general, both in agriculture and in industry, there was a very definite correlation between the number of workers available and the quantity of production. Insufficiency of agricultural production in its turn reacted upon the ability of the population to maintain itself. Taken together, all of these factors produced an overall condition of impoverishment which offers the fundamental explanation of the social and economic policy of the government of the Late Empire.

Undoubtedly, the ultimate objective of Diocletian and his successors was the preservation of the Empire. And it is equally beyond question that, with the exception of some weaklings in the West during the fifth century, the rulers of the Late Empire devoted themselves conscientiously and unsparingly to this task. It seems equally clear that for them the cardinal problems were the maintenance of internal order and the defense of the frontiers. Each of these problems required the presence of a strong, loyal, and efficient army.

Since the peculiar geographical situation of the Roman Empire, strung out as it was around the shores of the Mediterranean Sea, gave it frontiers whose length was out of proportion to its superficial area, and since the internal lines of communication were correspondingly extended as well as interrupted by the Mediterranean and its tributary waters, the size of the standing army had to be considerably larger than would have been required in a more compact state. Furthermore, the frontiers were under continuous attack or threat of attack from Persians and barbarians, so that, far from reducing the military establishment, Diocletian felt that he must actually increase it. The emperors of the fourth century tried to maintain the army at the level set by him, or even to strengthen somewhat its effectives. There could be no question of their reviving the citizen militia armies of the days of the Republic. They had to accept the professional, long-service army developed under the Early Empire, although they might and did modify its internal organization.

As has been seen, in trying to enlarge and maintain such an army the emperors were faced with a shortage of suitable recruits, caused in large measure by the decline of the rural population. Hence they found themselves on the horns of a dilemma. Either they could conscript Roman civilians for military service and so decrease still further production and the state revenues, or they could adopt and employ on a larger scale the policy initiated by Marcus Aurelius, followed by other emperors, and resorted to much more widely by Probus, namely, to make up the deficit with barbarians. It would be naive to think that the imperial government was blind to the dangers of such a policy. That they adopted it, is a clear indication of the acute problem of available manpower within the empire. It led, inevitably, to the gradual barbarization of the army, that is, to the predominance of the barbarian element both in the ranks and in the officer corps, even including the commanding generals. It led also to the wholesale settlement of barbarian colonies within the western provinces as feeders for the army. These groups were not assimilated into the Roman citizen body. A vigorous and expanding population could have absorbed them, but not the enfeebled and discouraged one of the Late Empire. Yet in spite of these settlements, shortage of manpower for the army continued and this, coupled with decreasing revenues, led the state to resort to the subsidization of actually autonomous, although nominally dependent, barbarian tribes as federate allies under the obligation to defend the frontiers. The inability of the Roman government to prevent the settlement of these allies as well as other invaders within the Empire, coupled with the passing of the command of the army of the West into the hands of barbarian king-makers was the immediate cause of the disintegration of the Western Empire.

I should be the last person to claim that the fall of the West Roman Empire can be explained solely in terms of a problem of shortage of recruits for the army. In an article published a few years ago I tried to evaluate the role of policy or, to put it otherwise, of the lack of astute statesmanship in bringing about this catastrophe. There I called attention to the way in which the eastern emperors prevented their military organization from being dominated by a barbarian element and reduced the menace of barbarian invasions, whereas their western colleagues were unsuccessful in trying to shake off these perils. One of the main reasons why the eastern emperors were able to accomplish this was that they found a source of recruits in the Romanized population of the East with which to counterbalance their Germanic mercenaries. That West Rome failed to do so adds still further testimony to the lack of manpower at its disposal.

It has been held by some historians that it was not scarcity of recruits but lack of military spirit among the Romans that caused the emperors to depend to such a great extent upon barbarians. No doubt, under the system of recruitment which was practiced there was a tendency for the landholder to supply recruits of inferior physique who lacked the necessary military qualities. No doubt also, there was a great deal of self-mutilation to avoid military service, and desertions were only too frequent. The reason why such a poor type of recruit was furnished by the Roman element is to be found in the lack of suitable men who could be spared from essential production, as well as in the indifference of the *coloni* and other hereditary working groups toward the fate of a government which seemed to them more brutal in its exactions than did the barbarians. The Gauls, however, made excellent soldiers and so did the Illyrians, only there were not enough of them. Vegetius, in discussing the deficiency of suitable recruits, gives priority to decline of population over aversion to military life caused by urbanization.

Not only did the emperors require a large standing army to support their authority within the Empire and to defend it against attack from without, but they also had to maintain a system of civil government adequate for the administration of justice and, above all, for the collection of the taxes requisite for defraying the military and civil expenditures of the state. Here, again, they were the heirs of a long tradition which had resulted in the growth of a highly centralized bureaucracy. It would have been futile to think of replacing this with some decentralized system that might have been less expensive but, from the point of view of the emperors, less efficient and less subject to supervision and control. As it was, the attempt to enforce the economic and social reforms and to extract as large a revenue as possible from the civilian population led to increased departmentalization of the bureaucracy and also to an increase in the number of the civil service employees. This coincided with the replacement of imperial slaves and freedmen in the office staffs by salaried persons of free birth, a policy which had begun under the Early Empire and had been hastened by the decrease in the number of slaves available. As I have pointed out, the extent to which this produced a drain upon the civilian population cannot be estimated, but it did, undoubtedly, add to the number of nonproducers and correspondingly increased the cost of government. This in turn made the burden of the taxpayers still heavier and, under the declining economic conditions, led to further impoverishment.

If these essential military and civil services were to be maintained, the necessary government revenues had to be assured. Consequently, the emperors must find a way of raising adequate taxes when production was falling off and the manpower required for production was decreasing. Diocletian, who initiated the economic policy followed and elaborated by his successors, attempted a twofold solution. He introduced a complete revision of the tax system which was intended to place at the disposal of the treasury a constant flow of agricultural produce through regular taxation instead of resorting to irregular levies, and, as a necessary corollary, he bound agricultural workers to the soil in order to prevent a decline in production. This step can be explained only in the light of a shortage of agricultural labor and the fear that this shortage would grow more acute through the flight of farm tenants and workers. In all probability the decision to collect all taxes on land in natural produce and to pay soldiers and other government employees in allowances instead of in money was made in part because of the shortage of silver money and the virtual worthlessness of the coinage then in circulation. But there was also another important reason, namely, the shortage in agricultural production which, combined with the depreciation of the coinage, had led to high prices and a general increase in the cost of living. As has recently been pointed out, the payment of salaries in kind protected the recipients against a rise in prices and also, when they had surplus allowances, permitted them to make a profit by selling on the open market. It is a mistake to think that there was any general abandonment of a money economy and a return to a so-called natural one. In this connection it should be recalled that Diocletian began, and Constantine I completed, the stabilization of the gold and silver coinage, and also that during the later fourth and fifth centuries the government was able to pay a certain number of its employees in coin instead of in allowances if they so preferred. Furthermore, taxes other than those imposed on farmland continued to be paid in money. The eastern half of the Empire, as is known, had large quantities of gold at its disposal, particularly in the fifth and subsequent centuries. Thus, it would be rash to conclude that currency shortage was a major factor in the collapse of the Empire in the West. Shortage of production was more significant.

At this point, it might be worthwhile to consider briefly the view that the decrease in agricultural production was due to a condition of soil exhaustion which affected the Empire as a whole. I am in agreement with those who reject this theory. Beyond all question Greece, the Italian peninsula, and Sicily had suffered greatly from soil erosion and consequent soil impoverishment, which was an important factor in the decline of agriculture and of the rural population in these areas. But no such condition has been demonstrated for the Po Valley, the Rhine and Danubian lands, Gaul, Britain, and North Africa, or even for Spain, although it is possible that it had begun to affect parts of that peninsula. In the light of present knowledge of soil conditions in the Late Empire, the shortage of agricultural products must be attributed largely to shortage of rural labor and a failure to develop improved methods of cultivation and improved farm machinery which might have compensated for the decrease in manpower.

The collection of the land taxes in kind had important consequences for the commercial and industrial classes of the Empire. Of itself, the handling of income in natural products did not create any new problem for the government. From the beginning of recorded history the governments of Mediterranean and Near Eastern states had been used to raising and disbursing revenues of this sort. They were thoroughly familiar with all problems of transportation, warehousing, and distribution. And Rome was no exception. One need only recall that the land taxes of more than one province had been collected in kind, that from the later days of the Republic the government had imported a large part of the grain consumed in the capital, and that the Romans had had abundant experience in collecting and transporting army stores on a large scale. Consequently, the increase in revenues in kind merely required an increase in the number of granaries and other storehouses, of ships, of wagons and pack animals, and of persons engaged in handling and transporting government stores. Since, however, a very large amount of the wheat, barley, wine, oil, and other agricultural products contributed as taxes would be consumed by the soldiers and civil servants stationed in the areas where they were collected, this increase in facilities need not have been very extensive. Under the Republic and Early Empire the movement of government goods had been effected by contracts with private individuals or groups of individuals and in the third century by contracts with special guilds, insofar as this was not taken care of by the widespread system of *munera* or obligatory services imposed on the municipalities of the provinces. In most modern states an expansion of governmental activities of a comparable sort would have been taken care of by private agencies competing voluntarily for the opportunity to secure government contracts. This would have occurred also at an earlier time in Roman history. But at the close of the third century there were not enough contractors with the capital needed for undertaking such contracts and not enough manpower available for carrying them out if they had been undertaken by companies or by individual businessmen.

Faced by this shortage of contractors and workers, the government resorted to conscription. By developing to the utmost the principle of public obligations incumbent on both persons and property, they bound to the public service the capital and the persons deemed essential in the collecting of levies of all kinds and the proper handling of the various sorts of government supplies. Thus, the municipal councilors, the corporations of shipowners and transport workers, as well as the similar corporations of merchants and others engaged in processing or selling grain, wine, oil, and various sorts of meat for Rome (and later for Constantinople), found themselves reduced to the status of involuntary government employees. As members of these guilds or corporations they were compelled to serve the state either without, or at best with inadequate, compensation.

The same basic factor, the shortage of manpower for public service, brought about the impressment of the members of the municipal corporations throughout the Empire and of their capital into public service. The immediate reasons might vary from one type of corporation to another, but in every instance the underlying cause was an actual or a feared shortage of personnel for services which the imperial government deemed necessary for the proper maintenance of municipal life or for the proper performance of the part which the municipalities had to play in the whole system of local, provincial, and imperial administration. This obligation was extended even to the actors' guilds, whose members were bound just as strictly as were the carpenters, masons, and rugmakers, who acted as the municipal fire brigades. The only distinction between the condition of these local guilds and that of those who served the needs of urban Rome was that their services were not so continuously in demand. Most of their *munera,* however, had to be performed without compensation. In addition, all persons engaged in trade and industry were subjected to an onerous tax collected in gold and silver money.

Another result of the shortage and uncertainties of production was the taking over by the state of the manufacturing of arms and armor and, to a larger extent, clothing for the army. This additional encroachment upon the field of private enterprise may have been somewhat motivated by a desire to maintain a government monopoly of weapons of warfare as a means of controlling brigandage and insurrection. But coming as it did upon the heels of the economic collapse in the third century, it finds its chief explanation in the inability of private manufacturers to supply government needs in this area of production. On the other hand, the state monopoly of the production of certain types of silk goods and of purple dyes was not so much the result of any shortage of production as of the desire to reserve for members of the imperial court and high government officials the use of silk garments and also of the purple dye which had come to be associated with autocracy. This was all in accordance with the policy of emphasizing the sacredness of the imperial household and the great gulf that separated the emperor from the rest of the population. Since the supply of silk in the Mediterranean area before the importation of the silkworm from China in the middle of the sixth century was very limited, the monopoly of the production of silk goods was easy to establish and maintain. Like the monopoly of the manufacture of red dyes from certain species of shellfish which seem to have become scarce, that of silk manufacture had little effect upon the economy of the Empire in the West. As has been seen, however, in operating these enterprises as well as the government arsenals and clothing establishments, the state encountered difficulties arising from a shortage of labor. In its desperate attempt to maintain production it felt compelled to resort to the imposing of a permanent hereditary obligation upon its employees.

Having traced the part of manpower shortage in determining the military and economic policy of the Late Roman Empire, I shall now consider the effects of this policy upon the population situation. Did it create conditions under which population, and with it production, could increase and prosperity be restored? The answer is emphatically in the negative. The restoration of more peaceful internal conditions by the early fourth century did unquestionably lead to a temporary improvement in agriculture in some areas and to the rise of some new urban centers. And this improvement would naturally operate as a brake upon the rate of population decrease. But, unfortunately, it was neither general nor sustained. The crushing load of taxation and obligatory government services proved too great for the producing classes to support. They did not have the wherewithal to raise and support families large enough to maintain, much less increase, their numbers from one generation to the next. Their lives were so burdensome that each of the obligatory occupation groups sought to escape from its status. The army, the civil service, and the clergy seemed havens of refuge for many. Farm workers tried to enter one of the town corporations or deserted their fields to swell the numbers of brigands or to join troupes of invading barbarians. Town councilors even sought to hide themselves as hereditary tenants on the estates of the great landholders. People of various classes took to the forests or the desert to avoid the eyes of government officials. The result was a still further decrease in the manpower available for private or public production. Under such circumstances the government reacted as might have been expected. It tried to tighten the system of controls by which it regulated the lives of the vast majority of the population. Law after law reiterated the life-long obligation of the individual to his particular class or corporation and its activities, the perpetual lien of the state, municipality, or college upon his property for financing the performance of its functions, the hereditability of his status by his heirs, the ban upon attempts to alter one's inherited condition, and the prohibition to change one's place of residence. But all to no purpose. Conditions grew steadily worse. By the early fifth century the area of untilled land had reached astonishing proportions, and many of the cities had become ghost towns.

But someone may raise the question, how is such a state of affairs compatible with the building activities of the emperors of the time, with the multitude of churches that arose in the fourth and fifth centuries in Italy and the western provinces, or with the opulence of the homes of the upper classes and the apparently easy circumstances in which they lived? How can it be reconciled with the maintenance of the free distribution of food for the city proletariat of Rome at the expense of the government? The explanation is not difficult. Insofar as the emperors were concerned, they were caught in the toils of tradition and felt that as far as possible they must live up to the standards set by their predecessors. A display of public munificence had to be maintained if an emperor were not to lose prestige in the eyes of his subjects. And loss of prestige might foster discontent and lead to the support of a rival. It probably never even occurred to one of the late emperors to abandon the distribution of free bread, oil, and wine to the Roman mob, however much that might have reduced government expenses and however many persons and however much private capital it might have released for profitable enterprises. No better proof is required of the influence of tradition in this respect than Constantine's granting of similar donations to the residents of his new capital, Constantinople. But, as a matter of fact, after the age of Diocletian and Constantine I, few great buildings were erected in the western part of the Empire, and even for the adornment of Constantine's own arch in Rome an earlier monument had to be despoiled. A large number of the churches of the time were remodeled pagan temples or were built from the ruins of public buildings no longer requisite for the decreasing population of Rome and other cities, nor did they compare in size or elegance with the great structures of earlier days. The wealthy aristocracy of the Late Empire was composed of inner circles of the senatorial order. They were the great landholders who furnished the higher officials of the bureaucracy and, to some extent, of the army. Their estates grew as the smaller proprietors were sold out by the government or handed over their properties to their more influential neighbors and became their serfs rather than face the imperial tax collectors. They, too, acquired abandoned lands which the government offered to any who could afford to till them, and who but the very wealthy could do so? The majority of them no longer lived in the cities but in large country villas, at times fortified, surrounded by their dependent serfs. There, relying upon their influence in the administration and even at times resorting to armed force, they could mitigate or defy the demands of government agents. These few grew relatively richer, as the middle classes were reduced to beggary and almost disappeared, and the poorer sank to even lower levels of wretchedness.

It might possibly be asked, Why did not the extensive settlement of Germanic people within the Empire reverse the downward population trend in the rural areas? Possibly it did in some districts and during brief periods, for the Romans in earlier times considered that the families of these barbarians were larger than theirs. In many places the new settlers were numerous enough to have the memory of their presence perpetuated in the names of rural communities. But there is no proof of any permanent beneficial effects, and even after the settlement of the larger tribes of barbarian conquerors, the downward trend continued. For this the following observations may offer at least a partial explanation. The Germans, like the other peoples of ancient times, had a high rate of infant mortality and a low average longevity, both of which kept down the rate of population increase. Furthermore, the lot of those who were settled as *coloni* on the properties of rural proprietors was little removed from slavery. Like the rest of the peasants attached to the soil, they came to feel the double pressure of the demands of their landlords and of the state, and their share of their crops was reduced to the bare subsistence level. This gave no encouragement to the raising of any large families, but it did encourage desertion of the lands to which they were in bondage. A life of brigandage or the opportunity of joining a band of barbarian marauders would seem infinitely preferable to the thankless toil to which they had been condemned. On the other hand, those who were settled in groups on state land with the obligation to furnish recruits to the Roman army found their young men taken in large numbers into service. Although these were permitted to marry, their life was not conducive to the raising of a numerous progeny and their average longevity doubtless fell well below that of those not engaged in military service. At any rate, the ever-increasing shortage of recruits indicates that they were not very prolific since, as will be remembered, the sons of soldiers and veterans came to be obligated to follow the paternal profession. In this connection it may be worthwhile to repeat that for some centuries after the settlement of the larger barbarian tribes—Visigoths, Burgundians, Franks, and so forth—within the former limits of the western Empire, no rise in population appears to have taken place.

Did the expansion of Christianity, with its higher standards of morality and greater stress on family life, have any influence upon the downward trend of population? The answer is that its effects must have been very slight. Christianity was at first an urban religion, and its spread among the rural population in the fourth and fifth centuries was relatively slow. So it came about that the term *paganus,* "countryman," was used to describe a non-Christian, a "pagan." The urban population, as has been seen, kept on declining along with the rural. It is true that during these centuries the West did not experience the rush of Christian men and women to monasteries and convents that characterized the East. But all the same, the favorable attitude of the Christians towards celibacy was just as notable in the West as elsewhere. And at this time the Christians did not in general favor large families, as is shown by Eusebius's explanation of the Christian attitude on the question.

And so, with declining manpower and increasing impoverishment, the Roman Empire in the West, unable to defend itself against disintegration from within and invasion from without, staggered slowly on to its inevitable dissolution.

W. L. Westermann

THE ECONOMIC BASIS OF THE DECLINE OF ANCIENT CULTURE

William Linn Westermann was born in 1873 in Illinois and was educated at the University of Nebraska and the University of Berlin. He taught at Missouri, Minnesota, Wisconsin, and Cornell before coming to Columbia where he stayed until his retirement. His special field of interest was ancient economic history, a field in which his expert knowledge of papyrology served him well. His most important works include Upon Slavery in Ptolemaic Egypt *and* The Slave Systems of Greek and Roman Antiquity.

No one will question the fact that there was, at the end of the period of ancient history, an immense decrease in the quantity and quality of the production of those human goods whose sum represents that all-inclusive thing which we call civilization. We are all agreed as to the area of the world's surface included in the sphere of ancient culture, namely, the ancient Mediterranean world. There is some divergence of opinion, however, in regard to the time at which the rapid decline in intellectual interest and vigor occurred. Far greater is the diversity of opinion as to the reasons which underlie this, the most tragic act in the drama of human development. The causes usually advanced in histories written in English may be summarized as follows: (1) the ancient system of slavery; (2) the decrease in population; (3) the ancient system of taxation; (4) the constant drain of precious metals to the East; (5) Christianity; (6) the infiltration of barbarians into the empire. There are a number of lesser causes which are cited here and there. These six, however, are the ones commonly presented as most important. Fortunately the old view of the moral degeneration of ancient society as a primal cause for the decline seems to have been pretty generally abandoned. I am, therefore, relieved of the necessity of refuting it.

An essential weakness of the old discussions of the causes of the decline lies in the fact that they did not sharply define the character of the catastrophe and the relative time at which it occurred. It is a matter of internal decay, a desiccation of intellectual vigor in no way

From the article by the same title in the *American Historical Review 20* (July 1915): 723–43.

induced by external circumstances and accidents. Its manifestations appear markedly after the principate of Trajan when the martial vigor of the Roman Empire still seemed unabated and its powers of expansion unimpaired. The intellectual bankruptcy of the ancient world is declared in the period stretching from about 150 A.D. to 300 A.D. From the time of Constantine forward we are in another intellectual world. It goes without saying that the process of decay, despite its sudden manifestation, was a gradual one. Posidonius of Rhodes stands out as the last great scientific mind which the Greek world produced. Isolated figures appear after his day, like that of Galen, court physician to the Emperor Marcus Aurelius, whose works echo reminiscently the tones of the great days and the ideas of the master minds. But the great days were past and the masters were dust.

In what ways can we specifically prove so illusive a thing as a decline in human intellectual vigor? Eduard Meyer has enumerated a number of evidences of the decline in his *Wirtschaftliche Entwicke-lung.* In addition to and in confirmation of the list which he gives there is much evidence that might be cited. The art of the age of Constantine is so vitally different from that of the period of the Antonines that the brilliant Polish archaeologist, Josef Strzygowski, was constrained to explain it as a recrudescence of the artistic canons and forms of the old Oriental art of Pharaonic Egypt. His explanation has not been widely accepted. But the fact of the tremendous loss in artistic conception and technique is apparent. It is best explained, since it occurs throughout the empire, as due to the depraving of Graeco-Roman artistic standards and output, a retrogression to primitive forms and viewpoint. The conventional types of the coins of the third century strikingly illustrate the decadence of art and the debasement of social life.

The falling off in the spirit of commercial enterprise is evidenced by the history of the trade of the empire with India. As proved by the finds of Roman coins in India the eastern trade flourished from the time of Augustus to that of the Antonines. It reached its greatest height about the last of the first century. Evidences of continued trade exist until the middle of the third century, followed by a lull which lasted until a revival occurred at the close of the fourth century. Another drastic proof of decline, which is often advanced as a cause, is to be found in the wrecking of the imperial administration in the third century which resulted in the rebellion and independence of exposed territorial units of the empire. By the weakness of the central authority these districts were forced to undertake their own measures of defense and administration.

The correct placing of the bankruptcy of ancient civilization is sufficient to eliminate two of the causes advanced to explain the intellectual poverty and degradation of vitality which succeeded upon the wealth of culture and splendid vigor of the great period of Greek and Roman life. The first of these is the barbarian peril, commonly formulated as the "incursion," "infiltration," or "invasions" of the barbarians. Before the time of Marcus Aurelius there had been no vital harm done by the barbarian invasions, such as had occurred in the third, second, and first centuries B.C. The Greek and Roman world had suffered "infiltration" from early times and had, as it always would have done under healthful conditions, absorbed these elements without pathological results. It was when internal disorders had lowered the resistance of imperial society, from 200 A.D. onward, that the barbarian invasions accelerated the process of decline and powerfully accentuated the hardness and crudity of life which other causes had long since prepared and produced.

The second force which may be eliminated as a destructive factor by the sharper definition of the primary period of decadence is Christianity. It is an impossibility to obtain any satisfactory statistics upon which to base an estimate of the relative proportion of the Christian to the pagan population of the empire even in the third century. Adolf Harnack's careful study of the evidence obtainable leads him to conclude that in 300 A.D. the percentage of Christians in the eastern portions of the empire fell far below one-half of the total population. In the West the proportion must be greatly reduced below that in the East. About 250 A.D. the Christian community in Rome, the oldest and strongest of the churches of the West, may well have formed between 3 and 5 percent of the total population of the city. The first traces of Christianity which the Greek papyri have brought us from Egypt are a few certificates made out to people who had officially proved that they were not Christians. These are of the year 250 A.D., in the time of the persecution under Decius. A business letter from a Christian in Rome to a brother Christian in the Fayum which mentions the Alexandrian Bishop Maximus falls within the years 264–282 A.D. This is all that we have upon the Christians of Egypt in the several thousand extant papyri preceding the persecutions under Diocletian. Until further papyri may have changed the impression left by this lack of Christian documents from Egypt before 300 A.D. we are not justified in postulating a large Christian population in that country. It is therefore impossible to assign to Christianity any marked influence upon the empire, either economically or socially, before 300 A.D.

The old belief that the growth of the ascetic ideal and monasticism affected the empire by withdrawing vigorous elements from participation in active life has, I judge, been entirely abandoned. This development, which is to be assigned to the fourth century, came much too late to be considered seriously as a cause of decline, even if the numbers of those affected ever justified such an assumption.

The theory of the drainage of gold to India in coin and bullion is based upon two statements in Pliny's *Natural History* and upon the fact that a number of finds of Roman imperial coins have been made in India during the past century. Pliny says (*Natural History,* VI, 101): "This subject [the route from Egypt to India] is worthy of attention since India in no year drains less than 50 million sesterces [550 million according to the corrupt text of Pliny], of our empire, remitting in goods which are sold among us at a hundred fold gain." Again he says (*Natural History,* XII, 84): "India and Seres and that Peninsula [Arabia] take away from our empire annually, at the lowest computation, 100 million sesterces. So much do our luxuries and our women cost us." This has been generally accepted as meaning that these sums—$2.5 million for India alone, $5 million for Arabia, India, and Seres—went out of the empire in coinage or in bar, although there is nothing in either passage which, in my judgment, necessitates this interpretation. On the contrary, in the first passage Pliny mentions the importance of the route from Egypt to India because of the trade which plied between them. Certainly the ships from Egypt went to India laden with goods, not money alone. If we accept Pliny's statement at its face value and reckon the complete sum for the period from Augustus to Antoninus Pius, we come to the conclusion that the drainage of Roman imperial coins to India was $750 million during the period of the height of the Indian-Roman trade. The sum seems quite out of proportion to the possible gold and silver supply of the ancient world. I cannot accept the passages of Pliny, in them-

selves of questionable interpretation, as sufficient proof of the drainage of imperial coins to India. There are no other authorities, so far
as my knowledge goes, upon which such a claim may be based.

Even in the pages of Pliny assurance may be had that the trade
with India was one of exchange of the products of the empire for
many forms of eastern goods necessary to the high standard of living
maintained within the empire. He states, for example, that India had
neither copper nor lead, and exchanged her gems and pearls for
these. He indicates in two places that the gain to the Roman merchants engaged in the Indian trade was large. A report has come
down to us of the exports and imports of northern India as they
passed into and out of Barygaza (Broach on the Gulf of Cambay).
The exports were onyx, myrrh, Indian muslins, mallows, a great deal
of coarse linens, nard, costus (a pepper-like spice), and leeches. It is
distinctly stated that these were goods destined for the empire trade.
An additional list of exports includes ivory, lycium (a medicinal plant),
silks, yarn, and long peppers. The imports passing into India via
Barygaza were: wines, chiefly Italian, Laodicean, and Arabian; copper
and tin; coral and chrysolith; cheap garments of every sort; highly
embroidered girdles; styrax (a gum for incense); honey clover; gold
and silver coins, which were exchanged with some profit for the local
coinage. The imports destined for the Indian king of that reign were
regal—heavy silver plate, musical instruments, shapely maidens, wine
of superior quality, costly garments, and a fine quality of myrrh. The
indications are that the export of luxuries westward into the empire
was met by a fairly equal amount of luxuries carried eastward from
the empire. Furthermore, the annual balance of credit, as indicated
by Pliny's statement of the great profit in the Indian trade, seems to
have been favorable to the empire's merchants.

In addition to the proofs given that there is no responsible authority behind the theory of a great export of money to India from the
empire, a number of other considerations help to make the idea
untenable. I have been able to trace but five important finds of
Roman coins in India, four of which are mentioned by Mommsen.
The fifth is a hoard discovered early in the year 1898 in the territory
of the Rajah of Pudukota. Unfortunately, I was unable to obtain a
copy of the *Coin Catalogue of the Madras Government Museum* in
which the finds of Roman coins in India are gathered together by Mr.
Edgar Thurston. The catalogue of coins of the Indian Museum at

Calcutta shows but nine Roman coins of undoubted genuineness, as against 118 Graeco-Bactrian, 10 Seleucid, 15 Greek, and 42 Parthian coins. The catalogue of the Punjab Museum at Lahore shows no Roman coins. It is surprising, not that Roman coins have been found in India at all, but that so few finds have been recorded. India at the present time absorbs large quantities of silver from Europe and America, probably a larger quantity in relation to its exports than from the Roman Empire in ancient times. This silver does not return, because of the immemorial practice of hoarding still prevalent in India. Yet we do not apply to England and America of today Mun's mercantile theory, that the economic well-being of a country is measured by the surplus in money derived from its favorable balance of trade with another country. No more should it be applied to the Roman Empire in its trade relations with India.

The disappearance of commodity money from circulation in the Roman world was due to hoarding within the empire. This is sufficiently attested by the hundreds of finds of coins in all parts of the empire. Hoarding was due, primarily, to the lack of deposit banks and was greatly increased when economic disorders began to appear in the second century and reached their climax in the third century after Christ.

It is quite impossible to regard the depopulation of the empire as a cause of decline in its culture. The reasons for this statement may be briefly given. (1) Our sources of information upon the population of the ancient world are exceedingly meager. Of the general census returns from the various parts of the Roman Empire we have only a few notices and their accuracy is very problematic. In other words we have no reliable statistics. We must be chary of making general deductions on the basis of statements of even the best ancient historians, such as Polybius. This attitude of scepticism is, of course, all the more essential when we deal with the historians who rank as secondary and tertiary sources of information. (2) Upon general considerations of the movements of population there is reason to believe that the total population of the empire increased steadily during the first century and a half after Christ. For the cities this is made probable by their areas, as shown by excavations upon ancient sites. For the agricultural districts during the same period, the time of the growth of the colonate, an increase, rather than a decrease, would better accord with the general theory of population and poverty.

Statistics are, of course, absolutely lacking. (3) The depopulation of the third and succeeding centuries is primarily a result of decline and only secondarily and in the culmination of disasters a cause.

For our knowledge of the numbers of the slave population of antiquity and the ratio of slave to free labor the same baffling situation exists as for the question of population. We have no statistics which may be trusted to give us an accurate picture. Consequently the field has been left open to speculation and to general impressions based upon the statements of the literary sources, which should be applied only to specific districts. Again it is Eduard Meyer who has given us a new point of view in his *Sklaverei im Altertum,* correcting the exaggerated and distorted picture presented during the worldwide anti-slavery movement of the eighteenth and nineteenth centuries. In the economic life of the great Oriental section of the Roman Empire, including Egypt, slavery never played an important role in agricultural life. In industry and trade slaves were found in the large manufacturing centers, but in limited numbers. Household slaves were a luxury of the rich.

In the Greek communities the rise of slave labor was a feature and a part of the development of "manufactory" industry. From the early part of the sixth century onward the numbers of the slave artisans increased in the cities like Corinth, Aegina, Athens, and Syracuse, which were the centers of industrial life. From the industrial centers the use of slaves spread into agricultural life, but it never became in Greece the dominant form of farm labor, as it later did in Italy and Sicily. In certain portions of Greece, as in the central part of the Peloponnesus and in the middle-western sections of Greece, slavery did not at any time gain a firm foothold. Even in the industrial centers we must not lose sight of the continued existence of free artisan labor, working as units in the hard competition with the capitalistic manufactories, which naturally preferred to use unfree artisans because of the lower production cost. There was no organization of labor for its economic defense. Consequently the picture is that of capital using that form of labor which it could obtain most cheaply and exploit most advantageously. It was the unskilled free labor, naturally, which suffered most in this competition of free workmen against slave workmen. The building inscriptions at Athens show that few slaves were employed in the building trades and that these worked as assistants to the free artisans.

In Italy and Sicily in the last two centuries of the Roman Republic the free peasant undeniably went to the wall in the competition with cheap slave labor employed by the landed proprietors. Special conditions peculiar to the Italian state under Rome's hegemony brought about this result. The conditions existing in these two portions of the empire have given rise to the popular exaggeration of the extent of slavery and the notion of its decisive results upon the ancient economic and social order. After the victory of Octavianus at Actium in 31 B.C. and the establishment of the *pax Romana,* the slave supply, which was largely that of wars of the Roman imperialistic period, diminished greatly. At the same time there was no change in the willingness to emancipate slaves, as evidenced by the emancipation inscriptions. For two centuries, therefore, before the great break manifested itself, slavery had been rapidly decreasing and a new type of labor, neither free nor slave, had been taking its place. The height of the slave system in antiquity was synchronous with the highest development of ancient civilization. The economic background for the decline of ancient culture was not slavery, but the Roman colonate.

It is certain that the breaking of the ancient economic and intellectual order of society was due primarily to causes within the Roman Empire. External relations had little appreciable bearing upon the great change. The faults to be found in the current ideas upon the subject are two in number: (1) the habit of viewing separately certain economic phases of ancient society which were inextricably interwoven and inseparable; (2) an insufficient knowledge of the greatest of the difficulties which faced the Roman Empire—the agrarian problem. Combining the information obtained from comparatively recent finds of papyri and inscriptions with the two important sources previously extant, the literary sources (including the Latin agrarian writers) and the Theodosian and Justinian codes, the course of the agrarian development becomes fairly clear in its general outlines. Many details must yet be subjected to intensive investigation and reconstruction. Of the extensive literature which has sprung up in the past twenty-five years upon this field of work two studies stand out prominently as fundamental, [Rostovtzeff's] book upon the Roman colonate and Weber's investigation of Roman agrarian history.

The statement that the Roman system of taxation was the cause of the shattering of ancient civilization is an obvious half-truth. It merely begs the question. Why did taxation, which is a necessary evil, cause the collapse? Upon whom did the burden of taxation fall? Why could not the burden-bearers endure the weight of their taxes? In like manner it has always seemed to me to be entirely futile to say that ancient civilization finally collapsed because the Greeks and Romans put money into beautiful municipal buildings and sunk their wealth in unproductive public works. The ancients, as well as we, had the right "to furnish to the spirit manifold relaxations from labors, taking heed of public games and festivals in their season, and of an attractive setting for our private lives. For the delight of these things day by day drives away wretchedness." The entire question of taxation, with the inquiry into the legitimate or illegitimate expenditure for public recreation, can only be dealt with in connection with the large problems of production. For the Roman Empire the question of taxation is largely a phase of the widespread problem of the organization and administration of the state domains.

The difficulties which invested this side of Roman administrative policy were, for the peninsula of Italy, the results of the early development of Rome herself. But in the provinces they were an evil inheritance of her conquests. There the roots of the difficulty were deeply embedded in the past development of the Greek states, of the Persian Empire, and the empire of the Pharaohs. When Rome absorbed Carthage, Greece, Asia Minor, Syria, Palestine, and Egypt she brought under her domain, accepted, and spread an economic order that was rapidly developing the seeds of its own doom.

When Alexander the Great conquered the Persian Empire he found that the land of Asia Minor outside of the cities was held either as domain land of the Great King or as great proprietary estates. Almost all of the land was apparently given over to nobles and priests, who had emigrated from Iran. Castles arose throughout the country which served as strongholds and as the residences of the foreign landholding nobility. A free native peasantry was transmuted into a serf population, bound to the soil. In general it is fairly safe to say that the midland of the Persian Empire was characterized by large landed estates held in fee from the Great King. This system probably had attained its characteristic features under the Assyrian Empire. Its origins may be traced deeply into the Babylonian period.

Especially in the Nile valley Alexander assumed control of an agricultural state in which the land had for ages been the farm of the

Pharaoh and the laborers his peasants, each enrolled at the definite place where he was called upon for his villein service. In trade and industry, as well as in agrarian production, the Pharaoh had been the one great capitalist capable of far-reaching enterprises. It is probable that the weaving and export of linen had at times been a monopoly of the Egyptian kings. The great mercantile expeditions into Yam (central Africa) under the Old Kingdom and those of Queen Hatshepsut into Punt were entirely royal enterprises. In Babylonia and Assyria, too, the influence of the royal storehouses upon industry and trade must have been overpowering.

Upon this form of land tenure and industrial production the ancient Oriental monarchies had reached a status of relative social equilibrium and stability during the last centuries of the second millennium and the first half of the first millennium B.C. The Persian rule of the empire of western Asia seems to have brought with it economic stagnation. The irrigation system in the Tigris-Euphrates basin declined, and the entire economic vitality seems to have been sapped, along with other causes, by the excessive demands of the local governors for taxation, which was paid in produce. As this economic system set and became rigid, the culture of the ancient Oriental world had become traditional and stereotyped. The result of the system was spiritual monotony and intellectual anemia.

Granting that Eduard Meyer has overemphasized the modernness of the industrial character of Greek and Roman economic life, the fact remains that his interpretation is, in its larger aspects, the correct one and the essential basis for any further discussion of the subject. It may be best to avoid misunderstanding in dealing with ancient Greek industry by abjuring the use of the terms "factory" and "factory hands," the connotations of which are so irretrievably modern. These reservations do not at all change the fact that we have in the Greek world, from about 700 B.C., the development of cities with a wide expansion of industry and transmarine trade between the far-spread Hellenic city-states such as, quantitatively, the world had never before seen.

The articles for export, especially vases, were made in the Hellenic industrial centers of the period from 700 B.C. in "manufactories." The "manufactory" was the workroom of some wealthy man who was often an importer of raw products. The part of his supply which he might not sell to free artisans was worked into form for the local or export market in his *ergasterion* by bought or rented slaves. The free artisans, too, whether working singly or in a group, at home or in a small shop, were certainly manufacturing for export as well as for local trade.

Recent archaeological activity and the scientific analysis of the vase types found in various parts of the Mediterranean world are gradually leading to an accurate and unassailable knowledge of the general spread of trade of the Hellenic city-states and the special spheres of certain industrial cities, as well as the overlapping of the trade of one city into the sphere of another. The increasingly commercial character of the external politics of the Greek states after 700 B.C. is a result of this free and active competition. Other characteristics of the commerce and industry of the "classic period" are the rapid spread of the use of commodity money and a very large relative increase in the size of cities. The Hellenic world, however, developed very unevenly in this respect and the industrial cities were largely confined to the coastal areas. Central-western Greece, Epirus, and Macedon did not share in the industrial evolution until later. Nor did the use of coinage in exchange ever develop in antiquity to the point of superseding entirely exchange and payment in *naturalia.* Yet the outstanding characteristics of the Hellenic world at its height, as compared with the economic world which preceded it and that which followed the decline of ancient civilization, are these: (1) large cities; (2) manufactories in these cities whose output was destined and used for a widespread export trade; (3) the use of commodity money in exchange.

The Greek system of land tenure shows a freedom of alienation commensurate with the freedom of trade and industry, except in those states which, like Thessaly and Sparta, were directly organized on the strict basis of a landholding citizen army and in which the citizen allotments were theoretically inalienable. Despite the fact that the citizen army of Athens in the fifth century was largely a corps of free peasantry, enrollment in the demes was even then quite independent of calling or domicile. Ownership of land was no longer essential for deme registration.

It was under such conditions of economic freedom that the Hellenic world developed its remarkable civilization, distinguished by that intensity of individual expression which still impresses us as so singular and so inspiring. In the fourth century, during the exhausting period of the inter-state wars, the insufficiency of the city-state financial policy, along with other causes, began to produce results ominous for the future Greek economic life. In order to cover the extraordinary expenditures incident upon continental wars, the city-states began to alienate their domains and those of the temples and to sink in the wars the surplus in gold and silver objects deposited as offerings in the temples. Working upon the ancient theory of the supremacy of the state, by confiscation of the property of the wealthy and the sale of their lands the states made insecure what had been the safest sphere of investment of capital, namely, the soil. The exercise of the sovereign right of the states in establishing bank monopolies hindered the promising development of private banks, such as were springing up in Athens. The difficulty of the food supply for the cities, continually growing in size, in a land which was dependent upon imported foodstuffs, became increasingly apparent. Capitalism had not yet grown to a degree that enabled private enterprise to cope with this problem. Indeed the lack of highly developed transportation facilities and the insufficiency of private capitalistic enterprise backed by a system of state credits, made the question of the city food supply one of the most serious which faced the Graeco-Roman world throughout its ancient history. The governments were forced into the grain business as the greatest entrepreneur. Competition with the state, which could fix prices as the needs of the case might demand, was difficult for the small grain dealer. The growing signs of the inefficiency of the Hellenic city-state financial policy in the fourth century, its inability to establish a sound state credit, its attempts to help itself over hard times by establishing temporary monopolies, and the disastrous results of such a policy upon the security and vitality of private enterprise, are well stated by Riezler in his pamphlet upon Greek finances and monopolies.

Into the civilization of the Persian Empire an entirely new idea was projected when Alexander and his successors founded cities after the Greek model at the junctures of the great highways from the Nile River to India. The heart of each of these city-states was the group of Macedonian and Greek soldiers, officials, and merchants, who formed the citizen body. The native population was herded in from the villages round about. So the cities arose quickly by the Greek process of *synoecism*. Their business ideals and methods must, at first, have been entirely those of Greece. From the outset, therefore, we have two antagonistic political and economic principles pitted against each other—on the one hand the Oriental serf-state working under a system of natural economy, on the other the Greek city-state with its coinage system and its traditions of political and industrial freedom.

The greatest administrative question which confronted the successors of Alexander in western Asia and Egypt was that of the conduct of their immense royal domains. The inscriptions give us their divergent answers to the problem. The Seleucids sold off large tracts of the royal domain, including the *laoi,* or peasants, and their possessions, to private persons or to cities, granting to the purchaser full title. These alienated estates were then attached to some city-state and enrolled upon its land register. The new land-barons took up their residence in the castles formerly occupied by the Iranian nobles, or dwelt in the cities as absentee landlords. The Persian form of land tenure was not materially changed by this innovation. As to the agricultural laborers it is presumable that, even upon the great estates privately owned, they were still serfs, but now city-state serfs instead of royal serfs, enrolled on the registers of the city-states instead of the registers of the royal domain. They had no legal freedom of changing their domicile, but were definitely attached, for purposes of taxation and administration, to their native villages.

The information upon the agrarian and industrial history of Ptolemaic and Roman Egypt is, thanks to the papyri, much more definite and satisfactory than that for western Asia. Under the Ptolemies all the land of Egypt belonged to the sovereign. It was divided, for purposes of administration, into *Ge Basilike,* or royal domain, and *Ge en Aphesei,* or land under grant. The royal domain was worked directly by the crown by means of royal peasants, *Basilikoi Georgoi.* The land under grant was worked by subjects who had possession, but not absolute ownership. It is necessary to fix clearly the fact that the ownership of all land in Egypt rested with the ruler, and that the mass of the native subject population, both the royal peasants and those who worked the lands under grant for their leaseholders, were increasingly bound to their villages, to their agricultural duties, and certain villein services due to the state.

Highly characteristic of the administrative industrial policy of the Ptolemaic regime is the development of state monopolies. In the

Greek city-states of the fourth century these had been temporary expedients, employed in time of need. Under the absolutistic rule of the Ptolemies the monopolies of the state were continuous, carried on in the interest of the fiscus, and covering some of the most important branches of industry. The oil monopoly included a monopoly of production, manufacture, and sale of oil. The banking system, also, was a complete state monopoly. In many other fields the king either had a complete monopoly or appeared as a powerful competitor to private enterprise. So the Ptolemaic king, like the ancient Pharaoh, appears as the greatest manufacturer in Egypt and the greatest merchant.

That part of the population of Egypt which worked upon the royal domains or in the royal manufactories and all those who worked under any form of lease from the state, comprised a distinct class, distinguished in the papyri as "those involved in the royal revenues." The actual laborers in the monopolies were direct serfs of the state and the royal peasants rapidly tended to become serfs. Both alike were bound to the places at which they worked, and were punished if they removed from that place. The royal peasants might at any time be called upon for compulsory labor on canals, in the state mines, or upon the royal transport ships.

Such is the picture of the economic and social situation in western Asia and Egypt when these lands were brought within the Roman Empire. In Asia Minor there were great royal domains, which the Roman state inherited, together with manorial estates and city-state territories. The mass of the agricultural population worked the land in a condition which certainly bordered on serfdom. In Egypt there was the state, the all-powerful Ptolemy at the top, holding an absolute monopoly of the land and of many lines of industry, and appearing as a strong competitor to private enterprise in other lines. Below him stood a middle class, including priests, soldiers, and large leaseholders, who were already growing to be a semi-official body. Below them was the great mass of the Egyptian peasantry and laborers. Imposed upon this social structure in the eastern lands were the Greek city-state foundations, with their free political life, free at least in their local activities, bringing with them the traditions of the old Greek freedom of commerce and industry. The wealthy men of these cities were absentee landlords whose estates lay within the city-state territory. For the taxes from these estates they were responsible. The Hellenistic period is further characterized by a continual increase in the use of commodity money as opposed to exchange in *naturalia.*

The agrarian history of the Roman Republic is too well known to require anything more than a reminding sketch. On the one hand appeared the tendency toward the building of large estates, which was founded in the system of leasing the *ager publicus* [public land]. Against this tendency stood the insistent democratic legislation which worked toward the division of the farmlands of Italy among the veteran colonists of the Roman citizen body and the Italian alliance under Rome's hegemony. This struggle to maintain the old freedom of general disposal of the state lands carried with it an attempt to put a limit to the use of slaves on the Italian estates. The story of the failure of the democratic land policy in the second century B.C. need not be repeated. The reasons for the defeat of the citizen peasant and the small farmer are well known. In the first century B.C. the mischief was already done. A few great landowners ruled the state and some part of the old peasantry had become impoverished proletariate. In 104 B.C. a political leader at Rome asserted that there were not 2,000 men in the state who had property.

The annexation of Sicily, Sardinia, Corsica, and Spain and the adoption of the principles of the agrarian policies of Sicily and Carthage undoubtedly had a powerful influence upon the development already mentioned in Italy. In Sicily under the Syracusan hegemony a unified and simple system had been adopted in which all the land, whether city-state territory or royal domain, was treated alike. The sovereignty of the state was preeminent, all subjects were regarded as *Georgoi,* and all paid the tithe from their lands, just as the royal domains did. In this system the city-states had become administrative units in the process of bringing in the *tributum.* All the landholders of Sicily were regarded by the Romans as "*coloni* and peasants of the Roman people."

Upon the great African and Sicilian estates the laborers were largely slaves during the period of the Roman Republic. Free labor was used chiefly at the time of the harvest. In the West, therefore, the small farmer and agricultural laborer was forced into the city, there to seek subsistence in the city's industrial life or to swell the numbers of the poverty-stricken city proletariate. The founding of agricultural colonies as an outlet for this element had practically ceased after the defeat of the Gracchan legislation. The problem of feeding this element of the city population added to the difficulty, always so apparent in antiquity, of the city food supply.

During the first century and a half of the Roman Empire the Greek policy of city foundations spread into the West. With their growth manufactories arose. Their industrial life and financial system were those of the Hellenistic cities. For the taxes and liturgies demanded by the government the well-to-do citizens, chiefly the owners and lessees of agricultural estates, were held responsible. The *pax Romana* of the early imperial period closed the sources of the supply of cheap slaves. The numbers of the slaves decreased in agricultural labor because the prices paid for them rose so high that their use became economically disadvantageous. In the households of the wealthy, slaves still appear, of course; but they are luxuries which could only be afforded for personal service by the rich. In the industries slave artisans were still used side by side with free skilled laborers, as capitalistic investments of their owners to whom the proceeds of their labor went.

Beside the increase in the number of cities and their population, appears an immense increase in the imperial domains in the first century of our era. Those private estates which survived also grew to large proportions. But the smaller estates and leaseholds began to disappear rapidly. The place of slave labor upon these domains and great estates is taken by the *coloni,* who work the soil under a form of sublease for private owners or large leaseholders. The pressure upon them is always greater and the application of the doctrine of *origo,* the doctrine that they must remain fixed to the place of their registration upon the state books for the fulfillment of their services, is increasingly more strict. This theory is applied by the state upon the big private *latifundia* [estates] as well as upon the imperial domains which the government leased to the *conductores.* These leaseholders, who during the first century were absentee landlords living in the cities, were responsible to the state for the rentals, whether in money or produce, and the government sacrificed to them the *coloni,* or sublessees. The results upon the volume of agricultural production could not be otherwise than bad; and this is clearly apparent in the imperial legislation of the end of the first and the course of the second century.

The first of the Roman emperors to legislate against this vicious trend of affairs was, in all probability, Vespasian, who was the grandson of a minor tax official and son of a money-lender. From the time of the Flavians to that of Caracalla we have imperial decrees upon the relations of the *coloni,* or small leaseholders and the actual peasants, to the large leaseholders (*conductores*) and the great private landlords. This legislation speaks eloquently of the decline in production, the waste lands, and abandoned lands. It attempted to protect the *coloni* from oppression by the big leaseholders and private possessors. It tried to encourage them to bring under cultivation the abandoned fields. But in so doing it drew the bands more tightly about the *coloni.* To meet the oppression of the big landlords the state fixed the amount of produce the *colonus* was to pay to the landlord and the number of days of his obligatory services, on the imperial domains and private domains alike. And that he might be assured the rights which the state guaranteed him he was forced to dwell within the domain.

The system of leasing the public domains spread into Spain, Gaul, and the lands along the Danube. The state mines were also handled in the same way and here, too, by the time of Hadrian the *coloni* had displaced the slave labor formerly employed. In this inability of the imperial administration to reestablish in the East a strong free peasantry, quantitatively and materially strong, and to maintain the old free peasantry in the West, lie the basic causes first of the economic, then of the intellectual decline of the Graeco-Roman civilization. Three results of this inefficiency to meet a great problem are clear and definite.

1. Its great result was the decline in intellectual vigor of the great agrarian population. For the free peasant of Italy and the West in general became a work-tool of the state and the great landowners, a work-tool bound to the place where it was needed. Private enterprise and initiative disappeared and the conditions which arose were those already depicted for the end of the Pharaonic regime in Egypt and the Persian Empire in western Asia. In this process the agricultural slavery in the West had undoubtedly played its part.

2. As the Roman Empire passed from its small estates, worked by slave and free labor, to its great imperial and private domains, the number of the free agricultural "production units" declined enormously. Consequent upon the decline in the number of these produc-

tion units came a great decrease in productivity and the taxpaying power of a given acreage of land. Consequently the state, in order to meet its regular and increasing demands for taxes, was forced to press upon the *decuriones,* who were the great leaseholders or land capitalists resident in the city-states. Under the ancient theory of state liturgies they, too, were bound to their city-state by the doctrine of *origo.* Early in the third century the *decuriones* undoubtedly could be forced by the state to return to the city-state of their *origo* with which their obligations to the state were bound. Thus, in the third century, the middle class, too, was forced to the wall under the weight of its liturgical obligations and the lesser estates fell away more and more and helped to swell the vast domains of single land barons who were strong enough to resist the pressure and force immunities from the government.

3. The establishment of the colonate brought about the economic ruin of the industrial city. It must be remembered that the background of the high civilization of the Greek world was the city-state with its manufactories and its political and economic freedom. This civilization and the industrial city out of which it grew were the heritage of the Roman world. Outside of its Eastern trade and a much smaller volume of trade with the Germans, the empire had no other foreign spheres of consumption. The bulk of the city production must be consumed within the empire. The welfare of that form of economic order, therefore, depended upon the possibility of selling the city production to a widespread capacity to buy. And the consumers must necessarily be the country population. The colonate, however, had destroyed the consumption power of the country districts through the vast shrinkage in the free units of production. This eventually led to the abandonment of the cities, which lost in attractiveness as their industrial vigor decayed. The debasement of the imperial coinage in the second and third centuries is undoubtedly to be regarded as an administrative effort to meet, by temporary expedients, the conditions arising from the great economic disturbances just depicted.

In the second century the reversion began from an industrial life based on a wide use of coinage to the more primitive conditions of payments in kind and exchange of produce. In the third century the signs of this reversion are much more marked. The big estates again took up the manufacture of the goods which they needed. So the great epoch of the industrial city-state is past and with it "the glory that was Greece and the grandeur that was Rome."

What I have tried to do is to show that it was the loss of economic freedom, even more than the loss of political freedom, which had such disastrous results upon private initiative and finally undermined the ancient Graeco-Roman civilization. I am not unaware that other causes beside those I have enumerated played their role in this great historic tragedy. Among those which may be suggested are the spread of city-state and imperial monopolies; the lack of a state system of credits commensurate with and able to support the intricate and relatively highly organized industrial and commercial life of the empire; and the problem of the city food-supply. These questions, like many others in this field of work, are still open to investigation.

W. E. Heitland
THE ROMAN FATE

William Emerton Heitland was born in England in 1847 and educated at Cambridge, where he later taught. His three-volume History of the Roman Republic *is still useful and his treatise on ancient agriculture,* Agricola, *has not been superseded.*

The growth and decay and dissolution of a great empire is a process that must arrest the attention of all who take an interest in the fortunes of the human race. And, so far as the history of mankind has yet been unrolled, there is no more striking phenomenon than the wonderful story of Rome. It has been said that into Rome the ancient world (the Mediterranean world) was absorbed, and out of Rome modern Europe was evolved. For not only are a number of European states descended from provinces of the Roman empire: the influence of Rome affected lands that never formed part of that empire, and are not popularly classed as "Latin" countries. Moreover, the in-

From W. E. Heitland, *The Roman Fate* (Cambridge, England, 1922), pp. 9–41, by permission of the Cambridge University Press.

visible hand of Rome is on us still in law, religion, and traditions, and European expansion has carried her influence far beyond the seas.

It is therefore natural that in a thoughtful age, when men are busy investigating present problems and curious in studying the past, convinced that no effect is without a cause, the story of Rome should engage attention. The why and wherefore of the great course of events, from the small beginnings on the Tiber to the vast aggregate ruled by Trajan, and so to the stagnation and shrinkage of the decline and fall, is a fascinating question. Many answers have been given, and good answers, setting forth the causes of Rome's rise and the causes of her fall. I am not now to attempt to add to these particular explanations, but to ask whether we cannot detect certain main causes operating steadily through the course of centuries, expressing themselves from time to time in differences of detail, but remaining all the time fundamentally the same. My aim is to reduce the sound particular explanations to a simplified form, and if possible to extract therefrom something in the nature of a generalized conclusion, valid as a statement of conditions applicable to humanity at large and not confined solely to the history of Rome.

This may seem a large and overbold undertaking, and perhaps the first thing necessary is to see clearly what it amounts to. Let me start by inquiring whether it may not be possible to discern certain great and unmistakable elements of strength in political societies, the presence of which promotes growth and well-being, while their loss or absence entails stagnation and decay. No distinction between ancient and modern is to the point here. It is a question of what experience teaches us, and the most modern societies have behind them the longest range of historical experience. The lessons I propose to extract are very simple; but it is the application of platitudes, not the platitudes themselves, that seem to me not devoid of interest.

As it will be necessary to use the term State in the course of this inquiry, it is necessary to say something by way of definition. For in dealing with the history of Rome we are constantly in danger of confusion arising from expressions that seem precise while they are really ambiguous. And the most important distinction is one based on consideration of size. Difference of scale soon produces a difference in kind. In the course of ages this truth has gradually received recognition in the development of representative systems. But in ancient times no such solution of the problem of government was reached.

Leaving aside mere tribal units, not combined as yet into any union worthy the name of State, we find only two kinds of states (a) a city with its territory, (b) great empires. In the former, power rests with those who are in the full exclusive sense the citizens, whether they are many or few in proportion to the population of the state. Their franchise is a definite thing, to which privileges and obligations are attached: its duties must be performed and its rights exercised by each citizen in person. Admission of aliens, resident or nonresident, to the civic franchise is normally rare, the civic bond being normally hereditary and religious in character. Under such conditions, states were inevitably small in area and lacking in numerical strength. As a system of political association, this plan was unsuited to survive, and in the end it failed. On the other hand, great empires built up by conquest rose and fell. But the overthrow of one empire by the superior force of another did not mean the extinction of a great self-conscious unit. Rather it was the transfer of so much human and territorial resources from the control of one autocrat to the control of another. The empire-units tended to grow larger and larger. Free Greeks might beat back the aggression of Darius and Xerxes: but their victories hardly shook the ill-knit fabric of the inorganic Persian monarchy. The Great Kings bided their time, and in the end profited by the internal antipathies of free Hellas. When the Macedonian directed the resources of a controlled Hellas against Persia, he did, and could do, no more than extend the system of great imperial units. Henceforth the large state, however ill organized, is the unit with a future before it: the small state, however well organized, is an anachronism. In the recognition of this fact, and in attention to the difficulties created by the rise of scale in political units, will be found a great part of the interest of the history of Rome.

Speaking then only of states large enough to render it manifestly impossible for their citizens to take a direct part in the work of government, we may distinguish three main types existing in modern times. We may then try to discover what elements of moral strength are common to them all, and in the process may perhaps find useful material, applicable in criticism of the complicated case of Rome.

The Unitary state may be defined as one in which the parts are merely subdivisions of the whole, not components, but subordinates. France, unified by suppression of the old component Provinces, and cut up into Departments, is the obvious instance of such a state. Its essential feature is not the centralized supreme government (which existed long before 1789) but the abolition of local privileges and customary rights and the establishment of uniformity and equality.

The Federal state arises from the union of units already in being, which are strictly component parts. The first step in its formation is a combination of territorially independent units, each surrendering some portion of its sovereignty for the common good. The union may grow by the adhesion of other sovereign units, each adding new territory. Or, if the original union possesses or acquires unoccupied territory, it may develop new members within its own boundaries. In any case, the position of a member within the union depends on definite conditions determined by voluntary agreement and expressed in constitutional law. Now it is impossible from the first to secure that all members of such a voluntary union shall be equal in population and resources, and the problem arises, how to recognize the claim of the several members to equality as units, while making equitable allowance for the superiority of some members to others as furnishing a larger share of the joint power and importance of the whole. The solution of this problem was found in America by the device of a Congress of two Houses representing the two principles: a plan which has stood grave shocks and has made the United States the accepted model of Federalism.

By the side of this model we may see, and must not ignore, a scheme of what I venture to call Pseudo-Federalism. It is that of Germany, formed under the late Empire, and continuing under the present Republic. It is in effect the union of unequal component parts, former states, which retain traces of their past independent (or virtually independent) sovereignty. But the vital fact is that one leading state does effectually control the whole, partly by its own strength, partly by the support of its satellites among the lesser states. This combination of Federalism and Hegemony may or may not prove stable in the long run. At present it seems to rest on the material advantages of "scientific" administration, of which individual citizens are on the whole convinced. Whether this conviction will prove strong enough to defy the assaults of classes and parties, industrial or political, it is not yet possible to guess. The German union, a reaction against obsolete "Particularism," but effected by force, is a contrast to the American union in both framework and origin. But that it means the asserted existence of a solid German nation appears no longer open to doubt.

A third clearly marked type is presented in the Conglomerate State, if I may coin the expression for convenience sake. The term is meant to imply that a political unit of large area has been formed by conquest or dynastic succession or by any means other than voluntary adhesion. Acquiescent submission to a central authority is the outward sign of such union. But the parts have this, and only this, in common. Separated from each other by differences of character, often by geographical position, they can only be taught to combine individual local self-consciousness with common mutual sympathy by a patient and intelligent government, able and willing to work slowly and continuously towards a definite end. Now the central government of such a state is almost inevitably autocratic in form at the outset and so long as the period of territorial expansion lasts. Cohesion and unity of direction are the only available means of guaranteeing the strength needed for a career of expansion. Hence the need of an Emperor: and, as a succession of competent emperors is precarious and in practice soon broken, the necessary development of Bureaucracy, the shadow of Autocracy. But the same human frailty that denies mankind a succession of wise autocrats is sooner or later fatal to a bureaucratic system. Efficiency itself may produce a temporary contentment, and contentment in turn may breed stagnation; abuses soon flourish in a stagnant system, and whatever has been gained by mechanical order is speedily lost. I do not think we can point to a single case of a bureaucratic government functioning as a successful reformer or sincerely and intelligently leading the peoples crudely incorporated in a Conglomerate state into the ways of true cohesion and sympathy. Certainly not that of imperial Russia. A power mighty for aggression under the Tsars, we now know that she was all the while rotting at the core, as corruption spread and vitiated the governmental machine. Hence failure and revolution, the end of which is not yet. But the revolution under Lenin is to be rightly viewed as the sequel of the premature revolution under Peter the Great.

It will hardly be denied that the chief element of strength in these, and indeed in all, communities is their solidarity. In proportion as this shows itself in a living loyalty and cooperation on the part of all citizens, the more effective is this strength. Even a mere acquiescent subordination counts for something, as it did in Russia. A docile satisfaction with their system, and pride in its achievements, gave steadiness to German patriotism. A belief that their government is a protector of the interests of the humblest citizen reinforces the sentimental patriotism of France. American self-confidence and pride needs no comment. But the difference between active and passive patriotism shows itself very clearly when a state is subjected to a great strain. We have just seen France stand and Russia fall. Germany, after an astounding exhibition of power, is not disorganized so far by defeat as to be effectually paralyzed: it seems that she carries on her former ambitions behind a veil. Meanwhile the United States Government, with their people at their back, feel competent to devise a policy for the whole world.

Nor is it less clear that, in order to make this solidarity real and this cooperation effective, the citizens of a state must have some practical means of expressing their will. For without their consent the consciousness of common interest and a common duty cannot be lasting: and a mere temporary agreement is no sufficient guarantee of continued strength. A Representative system, the organ developed by modern states, serves the purpose fairly well: the more perfect the representation, the less it is a sham, the more effectually it does so. Counting of heads is indeed a crude procedure, and unwise decisions do and will sometimes result. But on the whole the plan is a success, in particular as a preventive of revolution and civil war. To know for certain that they are in a minority is a cooling influence on even the most ardent fanatics, however strongly they may be convinced of their infallibility. These considerations do not exhaust the question. A popular vote may record a judgment, valid for the time, on a proposal duly submitted to it. This decides what is or is not at present "practical politics." But popular assemblies, whether primary or electoral, are not capable of calm and reasoned initiative. They need something on which to pass judgment, and this something is found in the competing programs of political parties. To place a given party in power insures the promotion, for a longer or shorter period, of measures of a certain tendency. This arrangement meets an obvious need, providing a body charged with the responsibility of normal initiative, without suppressing the action of individual representatives. Thus the electorate in a modern state is sure of having a policy on which to pass its final judgment by a majority vote. Thus peaceful reform is made possible. That the striking contrast between the complete representative system of the United States and the sham-system of Russia in recent years illustrates the above remarks, is hardly in need of words.

Nor is it necessary to argue at length in support of the view that even in electoral judgments a fair degree of intelligence must be required of electors. Even a sound view of their own several interests is something, and we must not ask too much of the ordinary voter. But Representation has this advantage, that the representative has "time to turn round," to become acquainted with the realities of the situation, and conscious of responsibilities that are ever subtly changing. Thus Representation operates as a check on the inconsiderate vagaries of popular electorates. If circumstances change, the intelligent representative must in duty reconsider his pledges: still more must the intelligent elector condone what may seem an unauthorized liberty on the part of his representative. An elastic harmony of this character is only possible in a highly educated community. This point is well illustrated not only in the case of the United States, but in that of Germany, where the representative system was clogged by rules artificially designed to lessen the effective value of the votes of the poor. Yet so thorough was the education provided by the expert government for all, that no serious inconvenience arose. Even now, in the hour of defeat, much of the effect of this careful training evidently remains.

I have now set out in brief outline what I conceive to be the chief elements of moral strength in great modern states, in virtue of which the community is able to make a good use of its resources and opportunities. The presence of these affords at least some security for justice and good administration at home and the power to pursue a successful policy abroad. So long as they remain unimpaired, their healthy functioning is a means alike of wise conservatism and timely reform. Looking back to the ancient world, I proceed to apply these considerations to the case of Rome.

In Rome we have from first to last to deal with a City as the vital center to which all Roman citizens by their franchise belong. It is very hard for a modern man to grasp the full significance of this fact. Rome differed from other ancient cities in the very important point of her treatment of aliens. Her very origin seems to be connected with incorporations, but tradition quite credibly records a long period during which common citizenship did not imply equality of privilege. That equality was at length reached, but only after violent struggles, is probably true enough. Also that equality in principle was never equality in practice; for a new privileged order, based on wealth and influence, took the place of the old nobility of birth. No democracy of Greek type was formed in Rome. Popular assemblies might be the depositaries of sovereign power. But they voted by groups (and these numerically unequal), not in one mass, and under such conditions as to render them normally ineffective (save for elections) as organs of the general will. And the expansion of Rome in Italy soon made them utterly unreal. For all citizens must come to Rome in order to vote in person, and distant residence made this impossible for busy men. That no solution of the difficulty by some measure of a representative character should have suggested itself to the Roman mind may seem strange, when we remember that it had gone so far as to admit aliens, even manumitted slaves, to citizenship. In so doing it had to treat old scruples in a liberal spirit. But it could not take the further step of providing that a citizen's voting power should not be in practice nullified by distance. To explain this limitation of view is not difficult, but would be out of place here. What we are really concerned with is the fact that no means of ascertaining the will of the actual majority of citizens was found in the Roman state, and that this first necessity of popular government became less and less practically possible in course of time.

Therefore we need not be surprised that popular control never shaped the policy of Rome. The Assemblies only meeting regularly for election business, were not capable of more than an intermittent and capricious action in other matters. The Magistrates, normally irresponsible during their year of office, could very seldom be called to account afterwards for misuse of their several shares of the once regal power. Only under the pressure of some great excitement could the popular will act steadily for a while and get something done. Tradition records the stubborn perseverance, year after year, by which the Commons extorted the concessions of the Licinian laws (367 B.C.). But it is recorded as exceptional. Now surely there was need of some state organ to maintain the continuity of policy without which Rome could never have risen to become a dominant power in Italy. Such an organ was found in the Senate, the most efficient

political body of the ancient world. It was always there, ready to sit at
the shortest notice, and could thus deal with urgent business. As a
body, it was permanent: the roll of its members was only revised
every five years, and a seat in the House was usually held for life. The
members were generally men who had held public office, so that
whatever knowledge and experience was available for service of the
state was collected there. Naturally the influence of the Senate grew.
From being the adviser of yearly magistrates it rose to be virtually
their director. From being preparer of measures for the decision of
the Assemblies, and from being entrusted by them with special powers in emergencies, it gradually assumed functions not assigned to it
by law, and during the great period of Roman expansion it became
the *de facto* guide and ruler of the state. The control of public
finance inevitably rested with it, there being no other body at all
competent to discharge that important function.

So long as the Senate remained a pure and patriotic council of
state, and the sovereign Assemblies generally acted in patriotic harmony with it, the grave defects of the constitution might not render it
unworkable. But the expansion of Rome added to the volume of
affairs calling for continuous management, and thus increased the
patronage and power of the Senate. The conquest and organization
of Italy, followed by the long struggle with Carthage, left the Senate
in possession of powers which it took over because there was no one
else to claim them. The wider foreign policy fell into their hands, and
to the outside world the Senate became more and more the representative of Rome. With the acquisition of transmarine dominions,
ruled as official departments *(provinciae),* came the power of ap-
pointment to honorable posts, which soon became lucrative. Individual ambition and greed developed fast under such temptations.
The standard of living rose and the race for wealth set in: and the *de
facto* power of the Senate was in the interest of its members turned
to account in granting opportunities of glory to be cheaply won, or of
enrichment at the cost of subject peoples. All these powers were in
strict law liable to be at any moment resumed by the Assemblies as
parts of the popular sovereignty, which was not openly challenged,
but foiled in default of exercise. Nevertheless they remained with the
Senate, for the interference of the Assembly on rare occasions was
too casual and capricious to have any lasting effect. When at last the
period of revolution began, it was indeed found possible to shake the

Senate's power. It was found impossible to establish any other civil authority in its stead, and events proved that the only force capable of ruling Rome was one possessed of the control of armies.

Thus the latter days of the Republic were days of party violence and bloodshed. Action and reaction, fitful and futile, left the problems of state unsolved and the state weaker, till Julius Caesar took matters in hand and made an end of the ruinous farce. It was high time that it was ended. As the Roman people could not express its will, and Assemblies were now normally mere gatherings of the idle city mob, corruption and force were the only means of influencing what passed for a popular vote. The senatorial nobility used these means freely, spending vast sums on bribery and shows, and not shrinking from employing their hosts of slaves to intimidate citizen adversaries. And the money needed to support these and other forms of extravagance was not to be found in Italy: it had to be sought in extortion abroad, at the expense of Rome's provincial subjects and client kings. The failure of the Gracchi showed that reformers could not rely on stable popular support in a struggle with the Senate, interested in present abuses: that the Senate, placed in power by the sword, could not hold its ground, was made manifest in the breakdown of the constitution of Sulla. In short, when the need of reform was most urgent, it was also most hopelessly impossible. Things had gone so far that no single act of legislation could be effectual, while steady patient work was beyond the range of practical politics: continuous backing was nowhere to be found.

So ended the Republic. The germs of self-government by the votes of citizens had been sterilized through the impossibility of expressing the popular will by direct voting in a state of large territory. The great state council had succumbed to temptation, and was rotten. The Augustan Empire or Principate succeeded as a necessity, veiling monarchic power, in essence military, under a great show of popular forms. Its unreal make-believe was an ingenious shift, but could not last. Bit by bit the disguise dropped away. Government became more and more bureaucratic in character. The civil wars of 69 A.D. betrayed the secret that the basis of imperial power no longer lay in the imperial capital. The center of gravity was to be found in the comparative strength of the great frontier armies. Administration more and more fell into the control of departmental experts, mostly oriental Greek freedmen, and attempts to substitute Roman knights for these clever men of business do not appear to have changed materially the working of the system. It had both the merits and the defects of a machine, and the defects at least did not grow less with time. For even the perfection of routine tends to become a hindrance to salutary change. Moreover this great central organization was operating in a vast area of passive provinces, from which no healthy constitutional stimulus could be received. The native peoples, long deprived of the power of independent action, had lost the will. Accustomed to look to Rome for guidance and orders, above all for their defense against outside invaders, they were politically dead. Even the internal differences of local communities were referred for settlement to the Emperor; that is, normally to his departmental ministers. The municipal system, by which the provinces were divided into lesser units not all equal in privilege, tended to promote particular interests. In some parts of the empire local jealousies were extreme, but the strong central power kept them in control for an outwardly prosperous period of some 200 years. No doubt evils were at work sapping the vitality of the imperial body; but signs of decay attracted little attention so long as the frontier armies were able to hold at bay the foreign enemies and preserve inviolate the Roman peace.

Then, in the third century A.D., after 200 years of Roman Emperors, came a time of disasters within and without, in which the evils long at work came to a head and the empire seemed to be on the verge of complete dissolution. Wars followed wars on the northern and eastern frontiers. Pretenders headed rebellions in various parts of the empire. Pestilence and famine carried off great numbers of the people and lessened available resources. The northern barbarians were stronger and more confident; and the armies employed to keep them in check were now largely composed of barbarian troops. The revival of the Persian monarchy led to a series of indecisive campaigns. Most emperors of this period spent their short terms of power at the head of armies in the field, and some were victims of the fickle soldiery who had lately raised them to the throne. The devastation of frontier provinces left the central government more dependent on the resources of those hitherto undisturbed, such as Africa and Egypt. We may fairly infer that these still flourishing lands had to bear an increased share of the economic strain. That the empire did not as a whole succumb under the pressure of its manifold burdens, is a marvel. We can only account for it to some extent by remarking that its external enemies were not united, so that it was still possible to make a stand against them in detail, and that their military systems were on the whole inferior to that of Rome. That the whole governmental fabric did not irretrievably collapse, is even more marvellous. Evidently an important page of internal history is lost. But we have a few detailed facts—enough to prove that among the confusions and calamities of the age the central administration did somehow continue in function. It still received appeals from the provincial subjects and gave judgment thereon. It could persecute the Christian movement as being a challenge to imperial unity expressed in the divinity of emperors. It could intensify imperial uniformity by wholesale extension of the Roman franchise in the famous ordinance of Caracalla. And it is above all things notable that the earlier part of this period was the golden age of Roman jurisprudence, in which Ulpian and other great lawyers flourished and often occupied the position of Praetorian Prefect, the head of the imperial civil service.

But in the latter part of the period the change really in progress became more manifest, the ruinous debasement of the currency was a symptom of the prevalent exhaustion, and the efforts of warrior emperors could not restore the empire's vital strength. A means of saving it for a time was found in the open recognition of a tendency already long at work, the transition to autocratic monarchy on an oriental model. Ceremony, display, formalities of an elaborate court, a graded hierarchy of official ministers, were leading features of the system. An emperor, secluded and almost unapproachable, issued his orders from behind a screen of obsequious subordinates: his household, his acts and words, his person, all were styled divine. To insure obedience and prevent rebellion, civil and military posts of command were reduced in scale and increased in number. These changes inevitably led to an increased expenditure, and therefore to an increase of the already crushing burden of taxation. And this taxation, owing to the deplorable state of the currency, was largely levied in kind. It was thus most cruel just when the power of payment was at its lowest; for in times of dearth a given quantity of corn represented a greater value. Such in outline was the new model of government devised by Diocletian and developed by Constantine. In order to satisfy competing ambitions, and to provide more efficiently for defense, the supreme authority was organized in four local divisions, each with a departmental sovereign. Provision was made for retirements, successions, and fresh appointments, in fact for every contingency save the failure of human nature under extreme temptation in circumstances of exceptional trial. So within 40 years Constantine emerged from civil wars as sole emperor. True, the system did not at once die out, but another 70 years found Theodosius ruling alone, after a stormy period of warfare largely defensive in character, and not permanently successful in repelling the barbarians, who were now swarming over the frontiers and indeed settling down in provinces of the empire.

After this last reunion we need not follow the political fortunes of the Roman state, the permanent division, the disintegration of the western half, occupied by barbarian invaders, and the continued existence of the eastern half whose capital was the new city of Constantine. It remains to sum up the lesson conveyed by Roman history from my present point of view. From first to last, from the small beginnings on the Tiber to the time when she ruled by the Euphrates and the Clyde, Rome never developed a political organ capable at once of continuous action and peaceful reform. Primary Assemblies, fitful and hampered, were never a practical expression of the sovereign people's will in a growing state, and territorial expansion soon rendered them ridiculous. The Senate was practical, but it was ruined by succumbing to the temptations engendered by its own success. Bloody revolution left the victorious army supreme. But an army, able to destroy, cannot create. It can only raise a chief to power, and this enables or compels him to found a monarchy. No make-believe disguises, however congenial to the Roman mind, could dissemble the truth for long. Monarchy, so far as our experience of human history goes, does not easily escape the alternative of becoming either bureaucratic or constitutional: mere personal autocracy is too toilsome, and breaks down through the insufficiency of human powers. Now the material for constitutional government had been destroyed at Rome by the course of her history. So the real ruler had to rule through Ministers, when he could find men suited to his purpose. But Ministers both capable and loyal were not always to be found, and Emperors were soon driven to transact imperial business through the agency of dependents of their own, men highly qualified but not of Roman origin. And the bureaucratic organization once established never died out. A great machine administered the empire. The vagaries of Emperors seldom and slightly interfered with its working. It tended to become more and more mechanical, a system of fixed routine modified by the corruptions of personal greed misusing the opportunities of official power. To us it may stand as a record, a confession that, whatever influence Roman tradition and sentiments may have had on government in past ages, such influence was now at an end. Stagnation and decay was the result.

From the political point of view let me turn for a moment to the economic. The early expansion of Rome in Italy was in essence an occupation, the work of the plow even more than that of the sword. The settlement of farmer citizens as owners and cultivators on con-fiscated lands gave solidity to Roman advances, while a judicious treatment of conquered neighbors on different scales of privilege minimized its difficulties and dangers. From time to time subject communities were admitted to Roman citizenship. The effective strength of the fabric, based on agriculture, was severely tested in wars with the invading Gauls, with Pyrrhus, with Carthage, and proved equal to the strain. But after the second Punic war things never returned to their old course. A "back-to-the-land" policy was at best only partially successful, and for this we may discern certain main reasons. These reasons may be generalized as the vital but imper-fectly understood relations of capital and labor. To set small-scale agriculture on its legs again, after the devastation of much of the best arable lands of Italy, needed fresh capital on easy terms; and this capital was not to be had. Men with money had learned to profit by opportunities during the great war, and were not now disposed to finance small farmers, even under the temptation of lucrative usury practiced with the aid of rigid law. There were openings for business of a less piecemeal character, and more tempting. Plenty of land was in the market at low prices. Plenty of slaves were to be bought, and no doubt fairly cheap. Contact with Carthage, and the spectacle of her remunerative and probably large-scale agriculture, scientifically managed beyond the standard of Roman experience, opened the greedy eyes of many. So two processes went on side by side. Men with money were buying up land and slaves, and forming large estates worked for profit by slave labor. Small cultivating owners were not returning to resume their interrupted occupation, or were actually driven to abandon the holdings on which they had main-tained themselves and reared their families. Some of these men preferred a soldier's life and served voluntarily in the subsequent wars. But many drifted into Rome and increased the population of the city. Rome was not a great industrial center, and progressive degradation followed. Eking out a precarious livelihood by the sale of their votes and general dependence on the bounty of the rich, they became a parasitic rabble. Courted by candidates for office, their perquisites grew: in time they were even fed by doles of corn provided by the state below cost price. Now this degrading process went on together with, indeed in connection with, the change in agriculture. The economic revolution could not be arrested by political action, because political power was steadily passing into the hands of the very men who profited by the new agricultural system. Politics could not be purified, because the remaining independent farmer citizens were not able to appear at Rome time after time in continuous support of measures for the public good. For we must not forget that the districts in which agriculture was being metamorphosed were chiefly if not wholly those easily accessible from Rome, not the uplands in which a scattered peasantry lived on.

For some 70 or 80 years the great change was at work before the capitalists won their final triumph in nullifying the efforts of the Gracchi. It seems to have undergone some modification in detail. Until the importation of corn from abroad became a serious factor, cereal crops appear to have been raised in considerable quantity by slave labor on the *latifundia*. But it was soon found that on these lines it was not possible to compete with Sicily and Africa in the Roman market, where sea-transport gave to foreign products, when bulky, a decisive advantage. Hence it was found advisable to devote landed estates to the cultivation of the vine and olive. And this department of agriculture implied a power of waiting for tardy returns, another advantage to the larger capitalist. It is probable that this change led to a reduction in the average size of large holdings, the new tillage being more intensive in character, needing more technical skill in the direction, and being (in the case of vines) largely carried on with use of the mattock and the spade. This modification seems to have been operative in the middle of the second century B.C., the time of the elder Cato. And there are signs that there was then still available some supply of free wage-labor. Such help was needed at seasons of special pressure, for instance the harvesting of crops. Thus it was possible to keep the costly slave-staff down to the number required for the ordinary routine labor of the estate. But it does not appear that any changes, abrupt or gradual, favored the return of the small farmer to the land. After the battle of Pydna in 168 B.C., which finally placed the Mediterranean world at the feet of Rome, the prospect open to Roman adventurers of all sorts was immensely widened. Provinces were being acquired, and further spheres of influence opened, and every forward movement brought with it alluring opportunities of gain. The next hundred years saw a great rush of Roman citizens abroad eager to exploit these openings. Some employed a temporary exile in gleaning the profits to be made by the legal or illegal squeezing of Rome's subjects. Others settled down in the Provinces or client kingdoms, and made fortunes by commercial or financial activities. In any case the power of Rome was at their back, and they used their opportunities with little fear of restraint or resistance. Extortion and usury were not the only means of enrichment. A Roman citizen enjoyed the right of *commercium,* that is of acquiring real property anywhere within the Roman dominions. The non-Roman had no such right valid in Italy. So bit by bit Roman emigrants acquired valuable lands in the Provinces, which they turned to account on the systems of cultivation in vogue. In a later generation the large provincial estates of Roman citizens were a very important feature of the imperial whole.

The foundation of Roman cities in the Provinces followed in due course, but the outflow of emigrant Romans, tempted by openings abroad, began at once. A man could make a start on a small scale, for instance by petty usury: the money-lender was an ever-present figure in the civilization of the time, and the favor of Roman officials guaranteed him against bad debts. The thrifty usurer soon became a substantial capitalist, and could choose whether to continue his investments abroad or to return home with the prestige of a man of property. And in Rome he enjoyed ample opportunities for deriving a good income from his capital. The system of undertaking state contracts by companies formed for joint-stock enterprise had received a vast extension owing to the current method of state finance. Revenues were farmed out by auction to the contractors who offered the largest lump sum down and took the risk of profit or loss on their collection. The growing volume of provincial dues brought into being a numerous class of investors, whose speculations generally yielded a rich return. From this class, known as the Knights [*equites*], little real sympathy with a disappearing peasantry could be looked for. At first their main object was to wring concessions from the Senate. So for a time popular leaders were able to engage their support against the ruling nobility; but the selfish interests of capital guided their policy, and eventually led them to combine with the senatorial nobles as a solid party of property. When we remember further that a principal department of commerce in the latter days of the Republic was the slave trade, in which Roman financiers were deeply interested, we need not wonder that efforts to restore free peasants to Italian land were a failure. Indifference or open hostility of capitalists effectually barred the way, even if the reform had been possible on economic grounds.

So the system of great estates and slave labor lasted on into the days of the Empire. It was found to pay well in Provinces where large blocks of land could be had at moderate prices, and where soil and other circumstances were favorable. Africa in particular was the scene of much enterprise of the kind. Now vast territorial units of this sort surely needed a very thorough organization, if the nonresident owners were to preserve an effective control and secure a regular income. And there is reason to think that the organization was, at least in many cases, very complete. So complete sometimes as to give to a great *latifundium* the air of a small principality, in which the private ordinances of the landlord were of far more direct and daily efficiency than imperial laws. But by emperors, concerned for their own security, the exercise of such authority by a subject was naturally viewed with suspicion. A decisive step was taken by Nero, who confiscated six estates of this class in Africa and thus added about half of that Province to the imperial crownlands. These imperial domains, administered by a central bureau in Rome, were already considerable, and tended to increase, and were an important part of the economic fabric of the empire.

Side by side with this process we must note another not less significant movement in Italy, and probably elsewhere also. Letting of farms to tenants was no new thing, but for various reasons only to be guessed it does not seem to have been a common practice. So long as slaves were plentiful, and landlords resident in Rome at the center of political life were content to draw from their estates such income as their managing stewards could furnish year by year, there was little inducement to have dealings with free tenants. Litigation was avoided, and with it the necessity of employing qualified legal agents to spare the landlords much trouble and worry. The Roman Peace of the Empire lessened the supply of slaves, while Rome as the political center lost much of its attraction for men who could no longer find free scope for their ambition in the strife of politics. It has been suggested, I think rightly, that the combination of these two influences led owners of land to reconsider their policy from a strictly economic point of view. At all events, whatever were the causes, we find indications of a marked extension of the tenancy system. That its success depended on a sufficient supply of honest and industrious tenants, steady and solvent, is obvious: and it was the deficiency of such tenants that soon caused trouble. Of the anxiety and losses of landlords we have good evidence, and it has been reasonably said that early in the second century A.D. they were often as badly off as their tenants. Yet tenancies in some form or other were, under pressure of circumstances, destined to be the prevalent feature of the agricultural system.

We have ground for believing that in earlier times the landlord had the upper hand in the bargain, and that the tenant was very much of a humble dependent, not in a position to refuse services required of him by his lord. His chief fear would be lest he should be turned out of his holding. In the younger Pliny's time the landlord was often the anxious party, fearing that good tenants would not stay while bad ones could not be got rid of without loss. Yet the social prestige of landowning remained, upheld by fashion. And estates in the Provinces seem to have been remunerative. It was now a problem how to combine two vital interests in such a way as to keep the agricultural system at work. For the production of food, always important, was now supremely urgent. The first point was, how to keep the tenant-farmer permanently attached to his holding, which could only be attained by giving him a prospect of decent comfort and prosperity. The second was, how to find room for the employment of capital in this great industry. We must not forget that imperial taxation in various forms was a general burden on agriculture outside Italy, and that it was an object so to collect the imposts as to keep down outgoings and keep up the net return. Out of the attempt to meet these requirements came a notable development of tenancy-practice, at least on great estates in the Provinces. A large unit of the kind was leased to a man of capital as chief tenant, who ordinarily kept in his own hands the principal or Home Farm, working it by slave labor under a steward. The rest of the estate was cultivated by small subtenants on terms which seem to have at least approximated to a common model. The chief tenant was responsible for the collection of imposts due from these subtenants as well as for his own rent. His existence was thus a convenience from the taxation point of view, and it was not unnatural that he should be allowed considerable authority. In particular it seems to have been the custom to give him a claim to services of the subtenants in the form of occasional labor *(operae)* on the Home Farm at certain seasons of the year. The need of such help to supplement the labor of his regular staff has been referred to above: it would seem that the arrangement was now passing into a recognized usage.

Whether, as has been suggested, this customary scheme first came into use on the great imperial crown-lands, or whether it began earlier on the Provincial *latifundia* of private landlords, we have hardly sufficient evidence to decide. Nor is the decision of first-rate importance. It is fairly clear that it was soon established on imperial estates and long remained in working order. Its interest here is to be found mainly in its observable tendency, judged by taking the witness of inscriptions (of second and third centuries) in connection with well-known later effects. That tenants-in-chief would try to get the most they could out of their opportunities, and that their subtenants would resist encroachments, was only to be expected. So it was, and strict rules had to be issued to regulate conflicting interests. These imperial ordinances were intended to protect subtenants against exaction of services beyond the fixed standard, and the chief tenants against shirking and fraud. No doubt the first object was the more important, for by this time the question of food supply was one of great urgency. But the enactment of rules was easy: to keep them steadily in force was difficult, owing to the corruption of imperial agents. These could, and sometimes did, connive at misdeeds of chief tenants, who were better able to bribe them than were the subtenants. Appeals from the latter to the central bureau at Rome were troublesome, probably expensive, and not certain of success. Success seems generally to have meant only a solemn reenactment of the rules. If, as may have happened, a corrupt official was removed, his successor was soon subjected to the same temptations, and the same weary round might begin again. In the confusion and disasters of the third century this system of contract-plus-checks cannot surely be supposed to have worked with purity and benefi- cence.

No wonder then that at the accession of Diocletian (284 A.D.) we find the small tenant farmer sunk into a semi-servile condition of dependence. The term *colonus* was fast putting on a new meaning. Starting from its original sense of "cultivator," whether owner or not, it had passed through a stage in which it connoted tenancy without ownership, the product of a bargain between two parties alike legally and economically free. The course of events had first embarrassed the ordinary landlord, and then gradually depressed the small tenant. The legal freedom of the *colonus* was now so clogged, and his economic position so dependent on the retention of a holding ham- pered by conditions liable to be impaired by piecemeal encroach- ments, that he was no longer his own master. To go was to starve, to stay was to become a serf. It only remained to recognize the situation by positive law, and the transition was complete. This step was taken by Constantine. Henceforth to be a *colonus* signified attachment to a certain plot of ground, together with which the farmer himself was legally transferable. This act, however logical, was really an act of despair. Stagnation in agriculture was now consummated by law, and the frantic efforts of the government to keep up or even extend cultivation could not extricate the empire from the economic mess into which it had drifted.

We can hardly shut our eyes to the conclusion that a potent cause of the decline and fall of Rome is to be detected in the fatal absence of any nonrevolutionary means of reform. From first to last (for we need not dwell on the details of collapse) good intentions on the part of individuals were nugatory for lack of any organ through which they could find effect. Whatever hope there might have been in the pure and clear expression of the popular judgment (perhaps not much) perished with the decay of a citizen peasantry; and the corrup- tion of politics sterilized all efforts at revival. The mechanical effi- ciency developed under the Empire was no remedy. It only served to conceal, and in some degree to retard, the decay of vitality. The real Rome was past, virtually dead, long before the monarchy became an oriental despotism. The point on which I am trying to insist is this: whatever particular evils tended to sap the vitality of the Roman state, we must bear in mind that there was no means of attempting to cure them by any effort of the human will. To contemporaries in Rome, as in all states in all ages, it was only the pressing evils of the moment that drew their attention and called for redress. A tranquil diagnosis, and a patient endeavor to remove the deep-seated causes of trouble, were impossible. In all states it is the strain felt by individuals that furnishes the motive power for any attempted reform: and individuals cannot wait. Therefore therapeutic measures are inevitably crude. And, however well meant or even well designed, they too cannot be instantaneous in effect. Still, given time, the experience of some improvement achieved may generate a readiness to wait awhile and watch for opportunities of carrying reforms further bit by bit, till at length a considerable result is attained. But such progress, I repeat, is only possible under a steady advance of public opinion able and willing to express itself freely in some regular and nonrevolutionary manner. Modern practice, fairly successful in spite of imperfections, supplies the needful machinery by submitting programs to electorates, who in turn delegate the function of final judgment to representatives who remain in session for considerable periods and so enjoy the advantage of time to reach calm and rational decisions. But in antiquity no such delegation of responsibility was known. The voter was himself an actual legislator. And there was no Ministry holding office until turned out, and therefore no Opposition bidding for office, putting forth rival "platforms" for mature consideration as competing schemes of party policy. The normal procedure was a popular vote for or against a particular measure proposed by this or that individual. Personal interests and passions naturally determined the result; which was, not to entrust the guidance of policy to deputies representing the majority, but to pass or reject a law by direct action of the voters present. I need not comment on the working of such a system in the little Greek democracies. Rome outgrew the possibility of drawing the greater part of her citizens to the Assemblies, and even in the Assemblies themselves the numerical majority did not prevail. No public opinion, organized and consistent, could arise among her widely scattered citizens. Popular sovereignty could only manifest itself in occasional assaults on the one practical authority, the Senate: and the Senate, whatever its merits, was not a body suited to undertake reform.

Therefore, if we detect evils undermining the strength of the Roman state, and find no successful efforts to remove them, we must surely make large allowance for the defects of a political system under which the noblest endeavors were doomed to almost certain failure.

Michael I. Rostovtzeff

THE EMPIRE DURING THE ANARCHY

Incomplete as it is, the picture which we have drawn shows very clearly the chaos and misery that reigned throughout the Roman Empire in the third century and especially in the second half of it. We have endeavored to show how the Empire gradually reached this pitiful state. It was due to a combination of constant civil war and fierce attacks by external foes. The situation was aggravated by the policy of terror and compulsion which the government adopted towards the population, using the army as its instrument. The key to the situation lies, therefore, in the civil strife which provoked and made possible the onslaughts of neighboring enemies, weakened the Empire's powers of resistance, and forced the emperors, in dealing with the population, to have constant recourse to methods of terror and compulsion, which gradually developed into a more or less logically organized system of administration. In the policy of the emperors we failed to discover any systematic plan. It was a gradual yielding to the aspirations of the army and to the necessity of maintaining the existence of the Empire and preserving its unity. Most of the emperors of this troubled period were not ambitious men who were ready to sacrifice the interests of the community to their personal aspirations: they did not seek power for the sake of power. The best of them were forced to assume power, and they did it partly from a natural sense of self-preservation, partly as a conscious sacrifice of their own lives to the noble task of maintaining and safeguarding the Empire. If the state was transformed by the emperors on the lines described above, on the lines of a general level-

From M. I. Rostovtzeff, *Social and Economic History of the Roman Empire*, 2nd ed. rev. by P. I. Fraser, Vol. I, pp. 491–501. Copyright © 1957 by Oxford University Press. Used by permission.

ing, by destroying the part played in the life of the Empire by the privileged and educated classes, by subjecting the people to a cruel and foolish system of administration based on terror and compulsion, and by creating a new aristocracy which sprang up from the rank and file of the army, and if this policy gradually produced a slave state with a small ruling minority headed by an autocratic monarch, who was commander of an army of mercenaries and of a militia compulsorily levied, it was not because such was the ideal of the emperors but because it was the easiest way of keeping the state going and preventing a final breakdown. But this goal could be achieved only if the army provided the necessary support: and the emperors clearly believed they could get its help by the policy they pursued.

If it was not the ambition of the emperors that drew the state ever deeper into the gulf of ruin, and threatened to destroy the very foundations of the Empire, what was the immanent cause which induced the army constantly to change the emperors, to slay those whom they had just proclaimed, and to fight their brothers with a fury that hardly finds a parallel in the history of mankind? Was it a "mass psychosis" that seized the soldiers and drove them forward on the path of destruction? Would it not be strange that such a mental disease should last for at least half a century? The usual explanation given by modern scholars suggests that the violent convulsions of the third century were the accompaniment of the natural and necessary transformation of the Roman state into an absolute monarchy. The crisis (it is said) was a political one; it was created by the endeavor of the emperors to eliminate the senate politically and to transform the Augustan diarchy into a pure monarchy; in striving towards this goal the emperors leaned on the army, corrupted it, and provoked the state of anarchy, which formed a transitional phase that led to the establishment of the Oriental despotism of the fourth century. We have endeavored to show that such an explanation does not stand the test of facts. The senate, as such, had no political importance whatsoever in the time of the enlightened monarchy. Its social prestige was high, for it represented the educated and propertied classes of the Empire, but its direct political participation in state affairs was very small. In order to establish the autocratic system of government there was not the slightest necessity to pass through a period of destruction and anarchy. Monarchy was established in actual fact by the Antonines without shedding a drop of blood. The real fight was not between the emperor and the senate.

The theory that a bloody struggle developed in the third century between the emperors and the senate must therefore be rejected as not fitting the facts. Certainly, the transformation of the principate into a military monarchy did not agree with the wishes of the senate, but that body had no political force to oppose to the emperors. Recognizing this fact, some leading modern scholars have attempted to explain the crisis in another way, but still in terms of political causes; on the assumption that the crisis of the third century arose not so much from the active opposition of the senate as from the relations between the emperors and the army. The new army of the second part of the third century was no longer the army of Roman citizens recruited from Italy and the romanized provinces; the elements of which it was composed were provinces of little or no romanization and warlike tribes recruited beyond its frontiers. No sooner had this army recognized its own power at the end of the Antonine age, than it was corrupted by the emperors with gifts and flattery, and familiarized with bribery; it felt itself master of the state and gave orders to the emperors. The conditions imposed by it were partly of a material, and partly, up to a certain point, of a political, nature: for example, that the privileges enjoyed by the ruling classes should be extended to the army. As the emperors had not succeeded in giving their power a juridical or religious basis which was sufficiently clear to convince the masses and the army without delay, it became increasingly clear that they governed only by the grace of the soldiers; each body of troops chose its own emperor and regarded him as the instrument for the satisfaction of its wishes.

This theory, which I hope I have summarized exactly, is undoubtedly nearer the truth and coincides in the main with the views set forth in this book [*Social and Economic History of the Roman Empire*]. I have shown how the Roman emperors tried hard to find a legal basis for their power. Emperors like Vespasian and, even more, Domitian saw clearly that the dynastic principle of hereditary succession, founded upon the Oriental conception of the divine nature of imperial power, and therefore upon the apotheosis of the living emperor, was much more intelligible to the masses than the subtle and complex theory of the principate as formulated by Augustus and applied by the majority of his successors, particularly the Antonines.

Yet the simplification proposed by Domitian could not be accepted by the leading classes of the Roman Empire, since it implied the complete negation of the idea of liberty, which they cherished so dearly. These classes fought against the transformation of the principate into an unconcealed monarchy, and in their tenacious struggle they had, if not as an ally, at least not as an enemy, the army composed of citizens who held to a great extent the same opinions as themselves. The result was a compromise between the imperial power on one side, and the educated classes and the senate which represented them, on the other. This compromise was effected by the Antonines. When, at the end of the second century A.D., the barbarization of the army was complete, that body was no longer able to understand the delicate theory of the principate. It was instead prepared to accept the hereditary monarchy established by Septimius Severus, and the emperor, with the army's help, was able to suppress without difficulty the opposition aroused by his action. So far I am in the fullest agreement with the theory described above.

But at this point difficulties begin. Why did the dynasty of the Severi not last, after it had been established, and accepted willingly by the army and unwillingly by the educated classes? How are we to explain the fact that the soldiers murdered Severus Alexander, and later even killed and betrayed the emperors they had themselves elected, thereby creating that political chaos which exposed the Empire to the greatest dangers? The continuous upheavals must have had a deeper cause than the struggle for the hereditary monarchy of divine right. This goal had been reached from the first moment; why did the struggle continue for another fifty years?

Perhaps the wisest course would be to be satisfied with this partial explanation, in the company of the majority of scholars. Our evidence is scanty, and the most comfortable way is always that of *non liquet* and *ignoramus*. In the first edition of this work I dared to offer a theory which is to some extent supported by our inadequate evidence, and which, if it proved acceptable, would enable us to understand the nature of the crisis of the Roman Empire. The five pages devoted to this explanation attracted the attention of the majority of my critics, and much has been written against my "theory," though without a single fact being adduced against it. The chief argument invoked against my "theory" is that the trend of my thoughts was influenced by events in modern Russia. Without entering upon an argument on this topic, I see no reason to abandon my previous explanation simply because I may, or may not, have been led to it by the study of similar events in later history. It still satisfies me and agrees with the facts insofar as I know them.

In my opinion, when the political struggle which had been fought around the hereditary monarchy between the emperors, supported by the army, and the upper classes, came to an end, the same struggle was repeated in a different form. Now, no political aim was at stake: the issue between the army and the educated classes was the leadership of the state. The emperors were not always on the side of the army; many of them tried to preserve the system of government which the enlightened monarchy had based upon the upper classes. These efforts were, however, fruitless, since all concessions made by the emperors, any act which might mean a return to the conditions of the Antonine age, met the half-unconscious resistance of the army. In addition, the *bourgeoisie* was no longer able to give the emperors effective aid.

Such was the real meaning of the civil war of the third century. The army fought the privileged classes, and did not cease fighting until these classes had lost all their social prestige and lay powerless and prostrate under the feet of the half-barbarian soldiery. Can we, however, say that the soldiery fought out this fight for its own sake, with the definite plan of creating a sort of tyranny or dictatorship of the army over the rest of the population? There is not the slightest evidence in support of such a view. An elemental upheaval was taking place and developing. Its final goal may be comprehensible to us, but was not understood even by contemporaries and still less by the actors in the terrible tragedy. The driving forces were envy and hatred, and those who sought to destroy the rule of the bourgeois class had no positive program. The constructive work was gradually done by the emperors, who built on the ruins of a destroyed social order as well, or as badly, as it could be done and not in the least in the spirit of destroyers. The old privileged class was replaced by another, and the masses, far from being better off than they had been before, became much poorer and much more miserable. The only difference was that the ranks of the sufferers were swelled, and that the ancient civilized condition of the Empire had vanished forever.

If the army acted as the destroyer of the existing social order, it was not because as an army it hated that order. The position of the army was not bad even from the social point of view, since it was the natural source of recruits for the municipal *bourgeoisie*. It acted as a powerful destructive and leveling agent because it represented, at the end of the second century and during the third, those large masses of the population that had little share in the brilliant civilized life of the Empire. We have shown that the army of M. Aurelius and of Commodus was almost wholly an army of peasants, a class excluded from the advantages of urban civilization, and that this rural class formed the majority of the population of the Empire. Some of these peasants were small landowners, some were tenants or serfs of the great landlords or of the state; as a mass they were the subjects, while the members of the city aristocracy were the rulers; they formed the class of *humiliores* as contrasted with the *honestiores* of the towns, the class of *dediticii* as compared with the burgesses of the cities. In short, they were a special caste separated by a deep gulf from the privileged classes, a caste whose duty it was to support the high civilization of the cities by their toil and work, by their taxes and rents. The endeavors of the enlightened monarchy and of the Severi to raise this class, to elevate it into a village *bourgeoisie,* to assimilate as large a portion of it as possible to the privileged classes, and to treat the rest as well as possible, awakened in the minds of the *humiliores* the consciousness of their humble position and strengthened their allegiance to the emperors, but they failed to achieve their main aim. In truth, the power of the enlightened monarchy was based on the city *bourgeoisie,* and it was not the aim of the *bourgeoisie* to enlarge their ranks indefinitely and to share their privileges with large numbers of newcomers.

The result was that the dull submissiveness which had for centuries been the typical mood of the *humiliores* was gradually transformed into a sharp feeling of hatred and envy towards the privileged classes. These feelings were naturally reflected in the rank and file of the army, which now consisted exclusively of peasants. When, after the usurpation of Septimius, the army became gradually aware of its power and influence with the emperors, and when the emperors of his dynasty repeatedly emphasized their allegiance to it and their sympathy with the peasants, and treated the city *bourgeoisie* harshly, it gradually yielded to its feelings and began to exert a half-conscious pressure on the emperors, reacting violently against the concessions made by some of them to the hated class. The *bourgeoisie* attempted to assert its influence and to save its privileges, and the result was open war from time to time and a ruthless extermination of the privileged class. Violent outbreaks took place after the reign of Alexander, whose ideals were those of the enlightened monarchy, and more especially after the short period of restoration which followed the reaction of Maximinus. It was this restoration that was ultimately responsible for the dreadful experiences of the reign of Gallienus; and the policy consequently adopted by that emperor and most of his successors finally set aside the plan of restoring the rule of the cities, and met the wishes of the peasant army. This policy, although it was a policy of despair, at least saved the fabric of the Empire. The victory of the peasants over the city *bourgeoisie* was thus complete, and the period of the domination of city over country seemed to have ended. A new state based on a new foundation was built up by the successors of Gallienus, with only occasional reversions to the ideals of the enlightened monarchy.

It is, of course, not easy to prove our thesis that the antagonism between the city and the country was the main driving force of the social revolution of the third century. But the reader will recollect the picture we have drawn of Maximinus's policy, of his extermination of the city *bourgeoisie,* of the support given him by the African army of peasants against the city landowners; and he will bear in mind the violent outbreaks of military anarchy after the reign of Pupienus and Balbinus, of Gordian III, and of Philip. Many other facts testify to the same antagonism between country and city. It is remarkable how easily the soldiers could be induced to pillage and murder in the cities of the Roman Empire. We have already spoken of the destruction of Lyons by the soldiery after the victory of Septimius over Albinus, of the Alexandrian massacre of Caracalla, of the demand of the soldiers of Elagabal to loot the city of Antioch. We have alluded to the repeated outbreaks of civil war between the population of Rome and the soldiers. The fate of Byzantium, pillaged by its own garrison in the time of Gallienus, is typical. Still more characteristic of the mood both of the peasants and of the soldiers is the destruction of Augustodunum (Autun) in the time of Tetricus and Claudius in A.D. 269. When the city recognized Claudius, Tetricus sent a detachment of his army against the "rebels." It was joined by gangs of robbers and peasants. They cut off the water supply and finally took the flourishing city and destroyed it so utterly that it never revived. The two greatest creations of the period of urbanization in Gaul—Lyons and Autun—were thus laid in ruins by enraged soldiers and peasants. One of the richest cities of Asia Minor, Tyana, was in danger of suffering the same fate in the time of Aurelian. It was saved by the emperor, and the words he used to persuade the soldiers not to destroy it are interesting: "We are carrying on war to free these cities; if we are to pillage them, they will trust us no more. Let us seek the spoil of the barbarians and spare these men as our own people." It was evidently not easy to convince the soldiers that the cities of the Empire were not their chief enemies. The attitude of the soldiers towards them was like that of the plundering Goths, as described by Petrus Patricius. His words certainly expressed the feelings of many Roman soldiers. "The Scythians jeered at those who were shut up in the cities, saying, They live a life not of men but of birds sitting in their nests aloft; they leave the earth which nourishes them and choose barren cities; they put their trust in lifeless things rather than in themselves."

We have frequently noted also the close relations existing between the peasants and the soldiers. It was through soldiers that the peasants forwarded their petitions to the emperor in the time of Commodus and Septimius as well as in that of Philip and Gordian. In fact, most of the soldiers had no knowledge or understanding of the cities, but they kept up their relations with their native villages, and the villagers regarded their soldiers as their natural patrons and protectors, and looked on the emperor as their emperor and not as the emperor of the cities. In the sixth and seventh chapters we described the important part played during the third century by soldiers and ex-soldiers in the life of the villages of the Balkan peninsula and Syria, the lands of free peasant *possessores,* as contrasted with the lands of tenants or *coloni,* and we pointed out that they formed the real aristocracy of the villages and served as intermediaries between the village and the administrative authorities. We showed how large was the infiltration of former soldiers into the country parts of Africa in the same century; and in describing the conditions of Egypt during that period we repeatedly drew attention to the large part played in the economic life of the land by active and retired soldiers. All this serves to show that the ties between the villages and the army were never broken, and that it was natural that the army should share the aspirations of the villages and regard the dwellers in the cities as aliens and enemies.

Despite the changed conditions at the end of the fourth century, the relations between the army and the villages remained exactly as they had been in the third. The cities still existed, and the municipal aristocracy was still used by the government to collect the taxes and exact compulsory work from the inhabitants of the villages. It was no wonder that, even after the cities almost completely lost their political and social influence, the feelings of the peasants towards them did not change. For the villages the cities were still the oppressors and exploiters. Occasionally such feelings are expressed by writers of the fourth century, both Western (chiefly African) and Eastern, especially the latter. Our information is unusually good for Syria, and particularly for the neighborhood of Antioch, thanks to Libanius and John Chrysostom. One of the leading themes which we find in both writers is the antagonism between city and country. In this constant strife the government had no definite policy, but the soldiers sided with the peasants against the great men from the cities. The sympathies of the soldiers are sufficiently shown by the famous passage in Libanius's speech *De patrociniis,* where he describes the support which they gave to certain large villages inhabited by free peasants, the excesses in which the villagers indulged, and the miserable situation of the city aristocracy, which was unable to collect any taxes from the peasants and was maltreated both by them and by the soldiers. Libanius, being himself a civilian and a large landowner, experienced all the discomfort of this *entente cordiale* between soldiery and peasants. The tenants on one of his own estates, perhaps in Judaea, who for four generations had not shown any sign of insubordination, became restless and tried, with the help of a higher officer, who was their patron, to dictate their own conditions of work to the landowner. Naturally Libanius is full of resentment and bitterness towards the soldiers and the officers. On the other hand, the support given by the troops to the villagers cannot be explained merely by greed. The soldiers in the provinces were still themselves peasants, and their officers were of the same origin. They were therefore in real sympathy with the peasants and were ready to help them against the despised inhabitants of the cities.

Some scattered evidence on the sharp antagonism between the peasants and the landowners of the cities may be found also in

Egypt. In a typical document of the year A.D. 320 a magnate of the city of Hermupolis, a gymnasiarch and a member of the municipal council, Aurelius Adelphius, makes a complaint to the strategus of the nome. He was a hereditary lessee (ἐμφυτευτής) of γῆ οὐσιακή, a man who had inherited his estate from his father and had cultivated it all his life long. He had invested money in the land and improved its cultivation. When harvest-time arrived, the peasants of the village to the territory of which the estate belonged, "with the usual inso- lence of villagers" (κωμητικῇ αὐθαδίᾳ χρησάμενοι), tried to prevent him from gathering in the crop. The expression quoted shows how deep was the antagonism between city and country. It is not improb- able that the "insolence" of the peasants is to be explained by their hopes of some support from outside. They may have been justified: the proprietor may have been a land-grabber who had deprived them of plots of land which they used to cultivate; but the point is the deep-rooted mutual hostility between the peasants and the land- owners which the story reveals.

I feel no doubt, therefore, that the crisis of the third century was not political but definitely social in character. The city *bourgeoisie* had gradually replaced the aristocracy of Roman citizens, and the senatorial and the equestrian class was mostly recruited from its ranks. It was now attacked in turn by the masses of the peasants. In both cases the process was carried out by the army under the lead- ership of the emperors. The first act ended with the short but bloody revolution of A.D. 69–70, but it did not affect the foundations of the prosperity of the Empire, since the change was not a radical one. The second act, which had a much wider bearing, started the prolonged and calamitous crisis of the third century. Did this crisis end in a complete victory of the peasants over the city *bourgeoisie* and in the creation of a brand-new state? There is no question that the city *bourgeoisie,* as such, was crushed and lost the indirect influence on state affairs which it had exerted through the senate in the second century. Yet it did not disappear. The new ruling bureaucracy very soon established close social relations with the surviving remnant of this class, and the strongest and richest section of it still formed an important element of the imperial aristocracy. The class which was disappearing was the middle class, the active and thrifty citizens of the thousands of cities in the Empire, who formed the link between the lower and the upper classes. Of this class we hear very little after the catastrophe of the third century, save for the part which it played, as *curiales* of the cities, in the collection of taxes by the imperial government. It became more and more oppressed and steadily reduced in numbers.

While the *bourgeoisie* underwent the change we have described, can it be said that the situation of the peasants improved in consequence of their temporary victory? There is no shadow of doubt that in the end there were no victors in the terrible class war of this century. If the *bourgeoisie* suffered heavily, the peasants gained nothing. Anyone who reads the complaints of the peasants of Asia Minor and Thrace which have been quoted above, or the speeches of Libanius and the sermons of John Chrysostom and Salvian, or even the "constitutions" of the Codices of Theodosius and Justinian, will realize that in the fourth century the peasants were much worse off than they had been in the second. A movement which was started by envy and hatred, and carried on by murder and destruction, ended in such depression of spirit that any stable conditions seemed to the people preferable to unending anarchy. They therefore willingly accepted the stabilization brought about by Diocletian, regardless of the fact that it meant no improvement in the condition of the mass of the population of the Roman Empire.

Michael Grant
THE OTHER WORLD AGAINST
THIS WORLD

Michael Grant was born in Sweden in 1914, and was educated at Harrow and at Trinity College, Cambridge. He has been Professor of Humanity (Latin) at Edinburgh University, first Vice-Chancellor at the University of Khartoum, and President and Vice-Chancellor of the Queen's University of Belfast. Among his many publications are From Imperium to Auctoritas, Roman Imperial Money, The World of Rome, The Climax of Rome, The Ancient Mediterranean, The Jews in the Roman World, The Army of the Caesars, *and biographies of Julius Caesar, Nero, Herod the Great, and Cleopatra.*

Hundreds of reasons have been suggested for the collapse of the Roman West. Some indication of their variety can be obtained from reading Edward Gibbon's *History of the Decline and Fall of the Roman Empire*. He lists at least two dozen supposed causes of that decline and fall—military, political, economical and psychological. Many of these "causes" will be referred to in the pages that follow. But the historian himself made no attempt to marshal them one against another, or choose between them. That is rather disconcerting for the reader who is searching for quick answers. But it also shows a good deal of prudence. For an enormous, complex institution like the Roman Empire could not have been obliterated by any single, simple cause.

It was brought down by two kinds of destruction: invasions from outside, and weaknesses that arose within. The invasions are easy to identify. . . . However, they were not sufficiently formidable in themselves to have caused the Empire to perish.

It perished because of certain internal flaws which prevented resolute resistance to the invaders: and the greater part of this book [*The Fall of the Roman Empire: A Reappraisal*] will be devoted to discovering those flaws.

I have identified thirteen defects which, in my view, combined to reduce the Roman Empire to final paralysis. They display a unifying

Reprinted by permission of the Annenberg Press and Thomas Nelson and Sons Ltd., from Michael Grant, *The Fall of the Roman Empire: A Reappraisal* (London, 1976), pp. 19–20, 291–308. Copyright © 1976 by The Annenberg School of Communications, Radnor, Pa., U.S.A. All rights reserved.

thread: the thread of *disunity*. Each defect consists of a specific disunity which split the Empire wide apart, and thereby damaged the capacity of the Romans to meet external aggressions. Heaven forbid that we ourselves should have a monolithic society without any internal disunities at all, or any differences of character or opinion. But there can arrive a time when such differences become so irreconcilably violent that the entire structure of society is imperiled. That is what happened among the ancient Romans. And that is why Rome fell.

*　　*　　*

If the pagans, and the products of their educational system, failed to meet the challenge of the crisis owing to excessively traditional attitudes, the great churchmen and theologians, men of superior brains and character who in earlier times would have been public servants, were guilty, too often, of a different but equally serious fault: that of discouraging other people from serving the state, either in a peaceful or a warlike capacity.

This had been a natural enough attitude in the old days when the state was engaged in persecuting Christianity. Their feelings at that period were summed up by Origen: "We Christians defend the Empire by praying for it, soldiers in a spiritual welfare much more vital than any in which a Roman legionary serves." In the same spirit, his more radical contemporary Tertullian argued that a Christian soldier in the Roman army who had refused to put a garland on his head during a pagan festival was entirely justified, even though his refusal might be followed by his own imprisonment, and by the persecution of his co-religionists. Indeed, the command to "turn the other cheek," attributed to Jesus, made it difficult for a Christian to be a Roman soldier at all; and there were numerous specific instances of men who, after embracing Christianity, felt unable to serve in the army any longer.

Nor was the Christian attitude to civilian public service any more favorable. For the scriptural saying "You cannot serve two masters, God and Mammon," was interpreted by identifying Mammon with the Emperor. "Nothing, then, is more foreign to us than the state," felt Tertullian. And the church Council held in about 306 at Elvira (Illiberis) in Spain declared that no member of the faith who had been appointed to an official post could be allowed to come to church throughout his entire period of office.

But it may seem somewhat surprising that, after the Empire became Christian, the church and its leaders, although they were now the partners of the Emperor, still persisted in their old conviction that Christianity was incompatible with state service. In 313, for example, the Council of Arles in Gaul pronounced that those who wished to take up political life were excluded from communion. For, in the words of an early papal letter to the Gauls, "those who have acquired secular power and administered secular justice cannot be free from sin." In consequence, a series of Popes, including Siricius and Innocent I, debarred those who had held administrative jobs from holy orders, explaining that this was because such government posts, even if not actually sinful in themselves, were gravely perilous to a man's soul all the same.

Moreover, this veto was still specifically extended, as in earlier days, to those who had served in the army. Indeed, the Christian leaders of the time, in spite of their new and intimate associations with the government, still continued to speak out frequently and openly against military service. Athanasius explicitly praised Christianity because it alone implanted a truly pacifist disposition, since the *only* foe it battled against was Evil. Basil of Caesarea related this attitude very rigorously to practical life, declaring that a soldier who killed a man in the course of his duties was guilty of murder and must be excommunicated. Even Pope Damasus, from his position of close alliance with the state, still praised Christian soldiers who courted martyrdom by throwing away their arms. St. Martin of Tours asked to be released from the army because "I am Christ's soldier: I am not allowed to fight." And when taxed with cowardice, he was said to have offered to stand in front of the battle line armed only with a cross. But then, according to the legend, the enemy surrendered immediately, so that no such gesture proved necessary.

Paulinus, bishop of Nola, supported these arguments against the profession of arms in explicit detail, contrasting it with the wearing of armor for God.

> . . . Do not any longer love this world or its military service, for Scripture's authority attests that whoever is a friend of this world is an enemy of God. He who is a soldier with the sword is the servant of death, and

when he sheds his own blood or that of another, this is the reward for his service.

He will be regarded as guilty of death either because of his own death or because of his sin, because a soldier in war, fighting not so much for himself as for another, is either conquered and killed, or conquers and wins a pretext for death—for he cannot be a victor unless he first sheds blood.

For those who were defenders of the tottering fabric of society, there is not much sign of any encouragement here. It remained for the unknown fifth-century writer *On the Calling of all Nations* to express, not merely the common belief that barbarians were the instruments of divine punishment, but the actual hope that Roman arms would *fail* against the enemy whose "weapons which destroy the world do but promote the grace of Christianity."

When such views were being expressed by bishops and theologians, it was hardly to be expected that their congregations would show any greater enthusiasm for the army and its tasks, however pressing these might be; and so the power of the Empire to resist its foes was sapped. Pacifism can only be pursued when no potential external enemies exist—and that was not the situation of ancient Rome.

Another menace to the loyal defense of the state was something more subtle. It came from Augustine, who possessed one of the best intellects of his own or any other age, and composed very numerous and abundant writings. Now Augustine could not accurately be described as a pacifist at all. The saying "turn the other cheek," he pointed out, can only be regarded as metaphorical, since to take it literally would be fatal to the welfare of the state. Wars were sometimes, he believed, a grim necessity, and might even be just, and in any case Jesus never told soldiers not to serve and fight.

Yet Augustine discouraged national service by more insidious means. Just as the monks undermined the Empire by physical withdrawal, so he undermined it, too, by a sort of spiritual withdrawal.

His work the *Civitas Dei*, rendered as the "City of God" though the word rather means "community" or "society," is not primarily a political treatise, but a work of theology. Nevertheless, its abundant pages yield important evidence of Augustine's influence on the political events of his time. Plato had described an ideal city which was the forerunner of Augustine's. It was "laid up somewhere in heaven," to be a model for actual communities upon earth. In later Greek times the Stoic philosophers had envisaged the world as a single unit, a cosmopolis, which is itself a potential City of God on earth, since all men possess a share of the divine spark. Then another philosophical thinker, Posidonius, turned this doctrine to the advantage of the Roman Empire, which he saw as the only realizable cosmopolis.

St. Paul, too, wrote that the minds of the enemies of Christ are set on earthly things, whereas Christian believers on earth "by contrast are citizens of heaven." Yet he held that earthly governments had to be obeyed, for they are instituted by God and are in the service of God, so that those who rebel against them are flouting divine authority. And in the same spirit the Gospels record a much-discussed saying of Jesus, "Render to Caesar the things that are Caesar's, and to God the things that are God's."

After the accession of Constantine, it was believed by his supporters that the words of Jesus and Paul enjoining obedience to the earthly power had become peculiarly relevant, since the unity between the heavenly and earthly communities detected by Posidonius had actually begun, under the reigning Emperor's auspices, to come about. Subsequently Theodosius I, by his total union between state and church, seemed to have completed the process, and the official doctrine was now insistent that by serving the Christian government a man was also serving heaven.

But when Alaric sacked Rome in 410, a wave of pessimism came over the relations between church and state. This gloom was based on certain antique attitudes. In particular there had always been a widespread pagan doctrine that the world, so far from exhibiting modern concepts of progress, was steadily declining from the Golden Age of the past down to the Iron Age of the present, with catastrophe to come in the future. Such doctrines, which conveniently coincided with Christian views of the Day of Doom and the Last Judgment, enabled Ambrose, for example, to take a most unfavorable view of the condition and prospects of the Roman Empire. After the battle of Adrianople, he announced "the massacre of all humanity, the end of the world," and then again in 386 he recorded "diseases spreading, time nearing its end. We are indeed in the twilight of the world." Christianity he saw as the crop coming just before the frosts of the winter: and the approaching world's end, as one of his followers explicitly declared, was to be preceded by the collapse of Rome.

Since the Romans, when they expressed over-optimism, were speaking foolishly, it seems hypercritical to denounce them when they were pessimistic as well. And, indeed, there was one thing to be said in favor of this gloomier attitude. It did at least appreciate that there was something terribly wrong. But useful plans to put it right were scarcely more apparent among Christians than among pagans.

Upon this world of unconstructive thinking burst Alaric in 410. Almost a century earlier, the Christian writer Lactantius had said that the fall of the city of Rome would mean the end of the world, and now, with Alaric's onslaught, both these events seemed to have come at one and the same time. "Eleven hundred and sixty-three years after the foundation of Rome," declared Gibbon, "the imperial city, which had subdued and civilized so considerable a part of mankind, was delivered to the licentious fury of the tribes of Germany and Scythia." Although, in fact, the Visigoths only stayed for three days, and did not do as much damage as might have been expected, this blow that felled the Eternal City seemed an appalling horror to optimists and pessimists alike.

Jerome, although far away in Bethlehem, took it as hard as anyone else. Alaric's earlier invasions had already filled him with the gloomiest forebodings, and now, after the sack of the city, he wrote to other friends in desperation, almost believing that the blackest prophecies had been right, and that the last days of the world were truly come.

> . . . I dare hardly speak until I receive more definite news. For I am torn between hope and despair, tormented by the terrible things that have befallen our friends. But now that this glorious Light of the World has been tampered with—defiled; and now that, with this city, the whole world, so to speak, is faced with annihilation, "I am dumb, and am humbled, and kept silent from good things."

Three years later, he was still reverting to the same theme.

> . . . Terrifying news comes to us from the West. Rome has been taken by assault. Men are ransoming their lives with gold. Though despoiled, they are still hounded, so that after their goods they may pay with their very lives.
>
> My voice is still, and sobs disturb my every utterance. The city has been conquered which had once subjugated an entire world.

Nevertheless, the Christian view remained equivocal since Alaric, in his work of destruction, seemed to be acting as the human instrument of God, and imposing a divine visitation, punishment, and test. "God's providence," wrote Augustine, "constantly uses war to correct and chasten the corrupt morals of mankind, as it also uses such afflictions to train men in a righteous and laudable way of life, removing to a better state those whose life is approved, or else keeping them in this world for further service."

Yet on hearing for the first time of the capture of Rome Augustine's first reaction, like Jerome's, had been one of deep shock. "Tidings of terror are reaching us," he declared to his African congregation. "There has been a massacre: also great fires, looting, murder, torture." Later he realized that these first reports were overstated. Acting with relative restraint, Alaric, himself a Christian, had spared the personnel and property of the church.

However, many people, and not only pagans, were asking why, since the Imperial government was Christian and allegedly enjoyed God's backing, had God allowed such a thing to happen. Nothing so frightful had ever occurred under pagan rule. It was in order to meet this challenge that Augustine began to write the twenty-two books of the *City of God*. "The first five," explains its author, "refute those who attribute prosperity and adversity to the cult of pagan gods or to the prohibition of this cult. The next five are against those who hold that ills are never wanting to men, but that worship of the pagan gods helps towards the future life after death." The second part of the work contains twelve books. The first four describe the birth of the two cities, one of God, the other of the world. The second four continue their story, and the third four depict their final destiny. These last twelve books contain a far-reaching philosophy of history which does not depend solely on Alaric's capture of Rome but possesses a universal application.

Augustine had read Plato's *Republic* in Latin translations, and had studied commentaries on the work. But he borrowed the concept of the two cities from certain contemporary North African Christians, the Donastists . . . who held that one city served God and his loyal angels, while the other worked for the Devil and his rebel angels and demons. At present, it was true, the two cities seemed inextricably mixed together within the church as in the rest of the world, but at the Last Judgment they would appear in manifest separation, one on

God's left and the other on his right, like the captor city Babylon and its liberated captive Jerusalem.

This vision of captivity and liberation excited Augustine and inspired him. And in consequence, during the years following 410, he began to develop this whole theme for his readers and congregations, elaborating it with the passion of a masterly and persuasive artist.

Two loves, he says, have created two cities: love of God the heavenly city, to the contempt of self; love of self the earthly city, to the contempt of God. The city of God is the city of the righteous, which contains God and his angels and saints in heaven, and all men and women who lead good lives on earth. The earthly city contains all unrighteous men and women wherever they be in the universe—fallen angels the souls of the unrighteous, the unrighteous in the world. Although, therefore, marginal points of contact exist, the earthly city is *not the same* as the Roman Empire.

What, then, does Augustine think of that Empire? The answer is founded on his doctrine of Grace. Without the god-given help to human beings, he feels that we who are lumps of perdition—sinful ever since Adam's Fall—can never attain eternal salvation. Augustine's own recurrent struggles between the flesh and the spirit caused him to share St. Paul's poor opinion of what a person can achieve by his own unaided will, and made him break with the more optimistic, classical, humanistic view that we can achieve great things by our own endeavors.

Augustine's attitude incurred the intense disapproval and anger of another Christian theologian of the day. This was Pelagius. Of British or Irish extraction, he came to Rome as a monk about 400. Like others, he was horrified by Alaric's sack of Rome, when "the mistress of the world shivered, crushed with fear, at the sound of the blaring trumpets and the howling of the Goths."

But Pelagius's reaction to such disasters was by no means limited to fatalistic gloom and despair. Both before and after the capture of the city, he found himself deeply dissatisfied with the moral sluggishness of many prosperous people of Rome. In an attempt to raise their easygoing standards, he insisted on a strenuous individual endeavor to attain salvation. He was convinced that the barrier of corruption which keeps original innocence and goodness out of our reach is insubstantial, and can be overcome by a bracing effort: we sin by a *voluntary* imitation of Adam, and an equally voluntary decision can cast our sins behind us.

The salvation to which Pelagius primarily referred was not of this world. Yet his doctrine was obviously applicable to worldly salvation as well—to the rehabilitation of the failing Roman Empire. If people bestirred themselves more and tried harder, it could be deduced from Pelagius, they would be better men. And that also meant, though he did not put it in such a way, that they would be better able to come to the rescue of their country.

This earnest belief in self-help caused him to abhor the tenth book of Augustine's *Confessions*, in which the writer repeatedly emphasized his dependence not on his own will but on the Grace of God. Pelagius himself, on the other hand, while not disbelieving in God's Grace, failed to see it as an overriding necessity. To him it was rather a form of divine assistance which can derive from moral exhortation and from a study of the supreme example of Christ: Grace, in this sense, will help us to fulfill and express the noble natures that have been bestowed on us by God. Like the earlier sort of modern existentialists before they became closely aligned with Marxism, Pelagius believed that man makes his own history on his own account.

Learning of this insistence upon the basic soundness and effectiveness of the human will, Augustine revolted against Pelagius even more violently than Pelagius had revolted against Augustine. He accused Pelagius of teaching, "like the philosophers of the pagans," that man by his own unassisted free will could achieve goodness without any help from God at all. Probably the criticism was unjustified, since what Pelagius really wanted to say was that heaven helps those who help themselves. But Augustine persisted in his censures for many years and wrote a treatise, *On Free Will*, endeavoring to strike what he felt to be a more pious balance between men's limited capacity for autonomous enterprise and his dependence on the divine power. In effect, however, the "higher freedom" which emerged, while professing to admit the liberty of the will, tended towards its annihilation as a well-spring of action.

Although Augustine's diffidence in his own powers (reflected in this formulation) displays an engaging humility, the doctrine of Pelagius was of greater value—on the practical plane of daily events and emergencies—to the later Roman Empire. It is true that he disliked the current spiritual inertia, and perhaps the whole social system that lay behind it, so much that he even spoke warmly in favor of monasticism. Nevertheless, his doctrine of the will at least wanted people to *try*. Augustine's philosophy, on the other hand, led to fatalism. Yet his incomparable eloquence, ably supported by many other preachers, ensured that it was his view which ultimately prevailed.

So Pelagius was doomed to failure. Jerome called him a fat hound weighed down by Scotch porridge, and he twice suffered excommunication. When and where he died is unknown. But after his death, the controversy continued with unabated vigor, and Gallic monks and theologians felt considerable sympathy with his views, for Augustine's increasingly vehement assertions of Grace as man's only hope seemed to undermine human effort.

Indeed, his pronouncements also carried more fundamental political implications, affecting the whole concept of the Roman Empire. For since man, he concluded, is so totally corrupted by the fall of Adam that he is bound at some time to sin, and even Grace cannot prevent this inevitable outcome; since, that is to say, for as long as he lives, he can never cease to be flawed, then all his institutions are flawed as well. Even the church, though it provides the only bridge to the heavenly city, remains a mixture of good wheat and bad weeds. How much more imperfect, then, must be the state, the Roman Empire itself!

True, although often perverted by evil wills, it is a natural and a divine necessity which God granted to the Romans. By his ordinance, continued Augustine, there is a king for temporal life, as there is a king for eternal life. Earthly rulers have special services they can render to God, just because they are rulers. And although Constantine was by no means perfect—for Augustine was one of those who believed that Christianity had lost virtue as it gained wealth and power—he paid honor to Theodosius I, as a prince whose devotion to the faith was exemplary.

When such men rule, one can see "a faint shadowy resemblance between the Roman Empire and the heavenly city." The state, in fact, has its uses. Love of our neighbor, felt Augustine, makes our patriotic and civic duties obligatory. Soldiers, rulers, and judges alike have to stay at their posts. And yet, all the same, we are reading the thoughts of a man in whom national feeling is so strictly and

totally subordinated to religious considerations that it can hardly, in
any meaningful sense, be said to exist. From the nationalist sentiments which had defended the frontiers of ancient Rome for so
many centuries we have traveled a vast distance. For example, while
granting that wars can be just and even necessary, Augustine concludes that their "victories bring death with them or are doomed to
death," and the vast extent of Rome's Empire, he adds, has given
rise to every sort of detestable foreign and civil war. Augustine even
says he would have preferred a number of small nations living in
peace to the monolithic Empire of the Romans. "Without justice," he
declares, "governments are merely great bands of brigands"—
gangsterism on a massive scale. But "without justice" is precisely
what, in the very nature of things, these states inevitably were: and
what Rome could not fail to be.

And so he preached, as others had preached before him, that "we
do not want to have dealings with the powers that be." That is frank:
it is a call to withhold service from the government. Equally frank is
his reminder that the Empire is bound to collapse anyway. "If heaven
and earth are to pass away, why is it surprising if at some time the
state is going to come to a stop?—if what God has made will one day
vanish, then surely what Romulus made will disappear much
sooner." Even the current identification of church and state will not,
cannot, suffice to stop the rot.

Where does all this leave the individual citizen? Rome, for his
benefit, has been firmly cut down to size. Our *real,* permanent fatherland, he is told—the only true kingdom, according to the strictest
idea of what is right—is elsewhere altogether. "What we want,"
states Augustine, "is a way to help us to return to *that* kingdom: that
is how we shall bring our sorrows to an end." As for all the earthly
crises and catastrophes, they can just be ignored—or even welcomed, seeing that God has sent them as a discipline. The calamities
of a country in which you are merely a foreigner do not really affect
your interests at all. When, therefore, such calamities appear, just
treat them as an invitation to concentrate your desires on things
eternal: and rejoice that your treasure is in a place where no enemy
has the power to approach. To a patriotic pagan, disturbed by the
disasters that have befallen Rome, Augustine spells out the message:
"Please pardon us if *our* country, up above, has to cause trouble to

yours . . . you would acquire still greater merit if you served a higher fatherland."

Those are not words that will impel a man to the defense of the falling Roman Empire. Augustine has shifted the center of gravity so that the state is now a good deal less than half of what matters: far from helping his country to survive, his attitude contributed to its downfall.

His implied suggestion that, since it was up to Providence whether the Roman world should collapse or not, human endeavor could do nothing about it in any case, met with the strong disapproval not only presumably of Pelagius, but of Gibbon. For the task Gibbon set himself was to show that it was not God's Providence but very real, earthly enemies and causes which destroyed the Romans: that "man is not trapped by history," as David P. Jordan puts it in his book *Gibbon and his Roman Empire*: "he does not live in a haunted house, he can emancipate himself through reason."

Although Augustine's full influence was not exerted for generations to come, subsequent writers during the last years of the Western Roman Empire were already echoing his fatalistic attitude. For example, it was perhaps now that the poet Commodianus positively gloated over the downfall of the city: "She who bragged that she was eternal now weeps to eternity." And in the words of Orientius, bishop of Auch in southwest France, "why go over the funeral ceremonies of a world falling into ruins, in accordance with the common law of all that passes away?" Moreover, Orosius, whom Augustine commissioned to write a history of Rome, not only reminds us once again that Rome deserved the German onslaughts—because in earlier days it had persecuted the Christians—but that these attacks will actually be beneficial, "although this may involve the crumbling of our Empire." Presbyter Salvian, who believed the same, added two realistic comments. First, the Empire was *already* dead, or breathing its last. Secondly, most Romans lacked the imagination to realize the supreme peril they were in: and if they did happen to possess such discernment, they lacked the nerve to do anything about it.

For the existence of this inertia—which is a very accurate diagnosis—the suggestion of Augustine that human endeavor could be of no consequence, either in this situation or any other, bore a share of the blame; or at least he very accurately represented a prevailing feeling. "Help from without," declared the zealous Samuel Smiles, author of that nineteenth-century gospel of work called *Self-Help*, "is often enfeebling in its effects, but help from within invariably invigorates." Help from within was precisely what neither the pagan nor Christian ethics of the later Roman Empire were able to provide: and the characteristic ideas of both faiths fell all too readily into line with the numerous other tendencies conspiring to bring about Rome's fall.

Ramsay MacMullen
MILITARISM IN THE LATE EMPIRE

Ramsay MacMullen was born in New York City in 1928 and educated at Harvard University. He has taught at the University of Oregon, Brandeis University, and, since 1967, has been Professor of History and Classics at Yale University. Apart from the works whose excerpts are included here, he has written several important studies of social history in the later Roman Empire, including Roman Social Relations, 50 B.C. to A.D. 284 *and* Roman Governments' Response to Crisis, A.D. 285–337.

The Roman army, being used for ends not strictly military, lost its professional edge in a process stretching over perhaps two centuries, first accelerated by Septimius Severus and never reversed thereafter. Partly as a result, but more because of the violence of the later Empire, civilians had to arm themselves for their own protection. Civilian turned soldier, soldier turned civilian, in a *rapprochement* to a middle ground of waste and confusion. By the process, each influenced the other, but one direction of influence, the militarization of civilians, was particularly significant, and did much to change society. Such in sum is what this book [*Soldier and Civilian in the Later Roman Empire*] tries to prove.

A comparison of Rome's military effectiveness at the start and at the end of the Empire is instructive, and depressing. In a battle of

Reprinted by permission of the author and publishers from *Soldier and Civilian in the Later Roman Empire* by Ramsay MacMullen, Cambridge, Mass.: Harvard University Press, copyright © 1967 by the President and Fellows of Harvard College.

five thousand legionaries against as many enemies, a spectator in Augustus's day would have had to give heavy odds on the Romans. Man for man, in physical strength and courage, Romans may have been no better than, say, the Gauls (whom Caesar eagerly enrolled); even in armament, their shields were too cumbersome, their swords too short, and their *pilum* something of an antique, and these in time were all improved or discarded. Still, they won their battles, by everything that distinguishes an army from militia: habits of command and obedience, morale, a superb supply system, and much else. That same spectator, however, four centuries later, would have found it a very even struggle between Romans and Huns, or Romans and Parthians. A Roman victory had become—such is the impression one has, from the accounts of the time—a mere fifty-fifty proposition.

The fault of the army lay not in its size. There were more troops under arms—or at least on the rolls—in 350 than ever before. Half or more of them were of the kind that Vegetius (1.3) so nostalgically endorses, country folk "ignorant of the baths, careless of luxuries, simple in mind, content with little." Such were, such rather should have been, the *limitanei,* encouraged by the additional consciousness that it was their own farms and houses that they guarded. Yet the *limitanei* were clearly looked on as second-class troops. Synesius is contemptuous of those in Cyrenaica, while the system of defense dependent on them alone, in one broad area of Tripolitania, collapsed after the middle of the fourth century. More might perhaps have been expected of the city troops. But Ammianus's account of the useless garrison at Autun, which required the support of veteran volunteers, is confirmed by Count Ursulus's somber apostrophe, as he surveyed the ruins of Amida: "Behold the spirit with which the soldiers defend our cities! These are the men for whose high wages the imperial treasury is exhausted."

Of the two kinds of soldier most numerous and typical in Ursulus's day, *limitanei* spent most of their time on their little estates, and, being as far as we know never drilled, taken on maneuvers, nor subjected to any regular discipline, they fought as we would expect, like amateurs. This is not to say that they were all farmers. If we may judge from the signs they have left, especially in Africa, they formed a shabby squirarchy in the frontier zones, semibarbarous, semisoldier, in forts that looked like houses. Their urban equivalents proved equally, but differently, inadequate. To them were entrusted, from the mid-third century, the cities newly walled and generally reduced in area; and here garrisons fell prey to diversions that Vegetius condemns: *balnea, deliciae,* and the rest. What is missing, of course, is something between farm life and city life, that is, the camp of the Antonine army.

That camp was never typical of troop emplacements in the East, where urban quarters notoriously prevailed, and in the West it was, after Diocletian, less and less built either for an army on the march or for a permanent post. Existing camps were abandoned, their shells left to pillage or to civilian squatters, or, with a fireplace in the antechapel, a latrine in the adjutant's office, children's sandals in the barracks, and sleeping quarters in the storehouses, they were remodeled to accommodate married men and their families. In some were included facilities—pens, troughs, stables—for domestic animals driven to refuge by the peasants round about. The most conspicuous achievement of Roman military engineers, Hadrian's Wall, being damaged in the raids of the 360s, was indeed soon repaired, but by efforts described as "clumsy botching."

When the army flourished, as under Hadrian, its habits remained reasonably pure. The largest contingents were forbidden to own farms outside or gardens inside the camp, "for fear that through the desire of cultivating the soil they may be withdrawn from military service." Off-duty guilds were banned as well as part-time trading and legal marriages. If troops had to be stationed in a city, they were divided from their hosts by an interior crosswall, suggesting at least a theory of separation, whatever the facts may have been. Septimius Severus, however, introduced very different policies: legitimate marriage for serving soldiers, permission to indulge in trade and usury, off-duty clubs for lower officers; or arrangements for swifter promotion, and for military careers borrowing greater brilliance from posts once reserved for senators. One can even see a lowering of the barriers between soldiers and civilians: liberal grants of municipal or colonial status to camp settlements, barracks abandoned or troops removed from camps into cities, as at Alexandria under Caracalla. It is not likely that these measures were the rash payment of political promises. The army was indeed the dynasty's chief support. It was also the only bulwark against the barbarians. And there were sober advisers able to deter Septimius, had he attempted to strengthen himself by weakening the empire in a merely selfish purchase of army loyalty. The emperor's council was, as a matter of fact, especially brilliant, and must have included several authors of treatises *de re militari*. What, then, can explain the deliberate tendency of the whole Severan family to soften the edge of military discipline?

The reason for the change most often given is the one just glanced at, the political needs of the Severi. Though much evidence supports this explanation, there is another fact that should be kept in mind, the difficulty of recruiting. Against the Marcomanni, Marcus Aurelius had armed slaves, against the Costoboci, Boeotian volunteers, against the Parthians, Spartan *symmachoi* and the *diogmitai* of townships and of private citizens. His son abandoned war, and raised legionary pay 25 percent. That was not enough. To keep pace with recent prices, Commodus should have managed an increase, not from 300 to 375 denarii, but to 800. Even the dramatic doubling of pay within the first twenty years of the Severi was inadequate. It had to be supplemented by those relaxations of discipline just described in order to make the service more attractive.

It should be remembered, too, how inflexible the Roman exchequer proved in any financial crisis. Emperors lived almost from hand to mouth, and any irregular expense had to be met by expedients—really, considering the grandeur and complexity of the empire, they are extraordinary—such as the invention of petty taxes, debasement of coinage, auction of the palace furniture, or, under a facade of political revenge, the harrying of the rich out of their properties. To the last, Septimius turned with enthusiasm. Even so, an increase of 100 percent in legionary pay, in his and his son's reigns, must have meant a permanent increase of 25 percent in the budget as a whole. The military and financial policies of the Severi must have reduced them to extremities.

There is nothing like bankruptcy to change a man's views. We cannot accuse Septimius of being naturally lax in his treatment of the army (later emperors confirmed the course he took), nor can we ascribe his policies to nothing but the payment of political debts. He and his advisers seem to have made a sober, fixed decision about the army which implied its general inadequacy, and which involved a major revision of the amount and mode of its payment, the conditions of its service, and the relations which must henceforth exist between it and its commander in chief. That this decision was based on economic considerations can be shown fully enough in the various attempts to make the army self-supporting, for example in the use of camp territories to supply their own troops with bread and meat. The evidence for the lease of legionary lands to soldiers, for the existence of legionary herds (attested by *pecuarii*), for soldiers engaging in businesses of their own and (under Alexander) for precursors of the later *limitanei* on a very large scale, all is predominantly or wholly Severan. If we look into other army needs—bricks, timber, arms—we are again met by Severan innovations, taking the form of factories in the West staffed and supervised by soldiers, covering acres and acres, firmly housed in stone buildings or in earthwork mills, and capable of a most impressive output. The object, autarky, is written large in these interesting experiments, some of which, such as legionary sawmills, apparently failed, others of which proved their value in a long history. Legionary bricks were sold in quantity to private individuals in the neighborhood well into the fourth century. Arms factories still existed in the fifth, managed by officers taken from the army. There were nearly fifty of them, spread throughout the North and East.

Autarky may have been a key word in the councils of the Severi. It was given to the army; it fitted the sweeping proscriptions of Septimius's enemies, by which he assembled such unprecedented crown domains; and the two together, army and crown estates, can be seen at work in a wide area in Africa, where new lands were reclaimed for agriculture and old lands defended by the cooperation of soldiers and *coloni*. Within the whole complex of imperial obligations, the army could play a further part. It could be used for building in the provinces, as had been done before, but as became more frequent in the late second and third centuries. It could be used in administration. A study of soldiers detached to the offices of civil magistrates, under such titles as *beneficiarii consularis,* shows a striking increase under Septimius which saved the cost of the freedmen and slaves used earlier. At the same time there is evidence for a very sharp increase in the use of centurions for police work in Egypt, and for *stationarii* as judges and tax collectors elsewhere.

These miscellaneous activities undoubtedly worked their effects on the men involved. Many, for their full twenty-five years, did nothing but write; many attended magistrates as messengers, ushers, confidential agents, and accountants, measuring their promotion from chair to chair, from office to office. It was surely impossible to withdraw such clerks to active service. Even within the legions, from Septimius's day, new duties made necessary new nonmilitary ranks—*actuarii, codicillarii, scribae*—and camp facilities for office work are fuller. When we add the police work of the soldier who "served nineteen years as guard" on an imperial estate, the specialization of the "camp nailsmith," or the pride of another who displayed on his tombstone only an engineer's compass and square, we have a total of very diverse, but certainly not very military, activities. They grew more and more common. From a mass of evidence, some fragments are especially striking: that a fourth-century writer could speak of "the soldiers who *usually* levied the taxes"; that a tax could become known simply as "the *primipilus*"; that a police force could be called "the Centurionics." Everyday speech is often revealing.

Two illustrations will be enough to show how involved the army might become in duties not properly its own. Both can be completely documented. We may take first the Egyptian end of the *annona civica*. A peasant sees at harvest time the tax collector attended by a soldier, who is present if necessary to enforce payment. So many bags of grain are handed over, taken by oxcart to a wharf (built by soldiers) on the Nile, and there put on board a barge. One or more soldiers go along as guards, and their expenses—wine, presumably, and food—are covered by a special tax paid upon lading. The grain is stored in the granaries of Alexandria, supervised by more soldiers; transported to Rome by a guild of shippers whose patron is a soldier; and checked at the capital by a *b(ene)f(iciarius) proc. Aug. annon.* and a *subcenturio*.

Or we may take, over a longer span of time, some hypothetical colony. Soldiers, needless to say, have conquered the land for Rome. They mark its extent with boundary posts, it is they who divide its territory into strips along a grid, and they trace its walls and its chief streets crossing at a forum. They supervise allotments and the tax status of each plot. The overall shape of the town is that of a camp. Some of them, as veterans, settle down in the richer sections, attract more of their kind, dominate the senate, and fill the town's magistracies. They fill, too, the reserved seats in its amphitheater (built by their subscriptions), enjoying a prominence merited by their wealth, their influence, and by the generosity they have displayed in a score of public monuments. From the town's birth to its maturity, soldiers have supplied the forming force. If, in the third century, it is attacked, soldiers again—not a garrison alone, but veterans who volunteer—will defend it.

Two other illustrations may serve for the reverse purpose, to show the approximation of civilians to soldiers. The most unlikely place to look is the Church. Yet in Antioch and Alexandria it had its own troops, on the eastern border it had "an army of monks" in turreted monasteries; a bishop and his deacon led the defense of Cyrene, and watched two brother bishops dispute the possession of an abandoned fortlet. In Cyrenaica the fortified church, in Numidia and Tripolitania the fortified church-storehouse, were common features; and throughout Africa and the East, religious strife invited churchmen to work hand in glove with the army, "raging around in company with Dukes and Counts," as the Council of Sardica said of Athanasius. If we look next at the city of the late Empire, we see it too, in desperate suddenness, building its fortifications out of pillars and tombstones, incorporating any great structure like a basilica or an amphitheater into its defenses, walling in an abandoned camp or walling out its very forum, and calling upon its youth and its veterans to form themselves into an army. Everything was done to make a city, in its gates, towers, and perimeter, resemble a fort, and if necessary an army engineer was called in to produce a more perfect transformation.

But this transformation is often too perfect. Ambiguous pictures of fourth-century *enceintes* in the manuscripts of the *Notitia Dignitatum* or in the mosaic of Orbe cannot be identified for certain as *civitates* or *castella;* clay models of a gate may belong to a city or a camp; the *castellum* and monastery, like the *centenaria* and fortified farms, are even to the eye of the expert literally indistinguishable. It cannot be known whether the Libyan *tribuni* of the fourth century are or are not in the army proper, or whether a bishop who is described as formerly *strateusamenos* was "serving" as a civilian or military "soldier." His services were in either case a *militia.*

One need not swallow Herbert Spencer entire to see, in this loss of specialization, in this slurring of the division between the professions of war and peace, a very serious degeneracy. Obviously a soldier who had a farm to look after, with tenants and flocks, or one who spent long terms of duty in an arms factory or at a grain depot, could not do his own job properly. A provincial senator called upon to organize a militia, to stand watches on the walls, or to improvise shelter for refugee peasants, was, just as clearly, not serving the normal purposes for which cities are assembled. These were the sins of omission, so to speak—specialization neglected. There was also the sin of commission, the intrusion of a man of one profession into another man's. It can be illustrated best for the soldier, who enjoyed great prestige throughout our period and encroached aggressively on civilian institutions. That this was utterly baneful no one today need be reminded. A Europe that has returned, in recent times, by route of brown and black shirts, to the medieval customs of livery and maintenance, has shown what happens when soldiers enter politics. The Roman equivalent was military patronage. Its growth can be traced easily and naturally in a number of fairly long and informative inscriptions of the third century that show officers as saviors in time of attack, and as temporary overseers of almost every aspect of local government. When to their legitimate position was added an estate in the country, wealth, blood ties with the local aristocracy, and the popularity of a benefactor, the military patron was almost complete. The only thing still to be mentioned was control of armed men, and that of course was always available to him. At the same time, the civil official was beginning to encroach on local government. He too was chosen more and more as municipal patron, he too was found concentrating his rich houses in the best parts of town, active on the side in usury and trade, and exacting from his lowly clients "great sacks of beans with which to sow his private acres." The private citizen, a magnate indeed but without imperial office, exercised *his* patronage by suborning troops and secret police from the state, or by arming his servants. These, however, are rather a feature of the fifth century. Under the name of *bucellarii* they are known in detail in Egypt. From three directions—soldier, civil servant, and private civilian—the armed patron emerges.

It is Septimius Severus who did the most to turn troops into odd-job men. His motives seem to have been mainly fiscal. A complete loss of specialization among soldiers is represented two centuries later by the commander of frontier guards. It is possible to imagine him owning some local fields in his private capacity, supervising the tenants of others officially, a man of standing on the countryside, living in his own fortified mansion, and, with his servants—some troops, some slaves or *coloni*—able to press his own olives, guard his own house from attack, or fend off the tax collector.

He may appear as the logical end of the Severan policies. Yet where the captain of the village is so nearly approached from other directions, the explanation for his rise must be a much broader one, concerning itself with the empire as a whole. Material for this explanation, well known, may be left to the general histories: unrest, fiscal oppression, barbarian invasions. The story of the Roman army is part of the story of the empire. Like that story, too, it is told slowly. The sluggish pace of change, traced here over some two hundred years, must be emphasized yet again. It is unlikely that contemporaries were even aware of its direction, however keenly they felt its results.

So much for the *"rapprochement* to a middle ground of waste and confusion." But it is also argued that only on this ground could soldier and civilian exchange the habits of life peculiar to each.

Civilian influence on the army is not easy to detect. In one broad sense it was complete, that is, the majority of the late fourth-century army was a mere militia. Its roots were in civilian life, rural or urban. More narrowly, the soldier as a soldier was little changed, indeed could not have been, short of fighting with a scythe in his hand or giving the orders of the day in hexameters. Some "civilianizing" may be seen in the architecture of the *praetorium,* which in the early Empire was already borrowing the general plan and inner comforts of a private villa. Another instance of the same process was the adaptation of parts of the camp to ceremonial purposes, and ultimately to worship. High officers did fight, or communicate with their men in their proper capacity, differently in the fourth century than they had done in the first. But the sum of all this is not very significant.

On the other hand, the influence of the army on civil institutions was profound. While the military way of doing things was perhaps no better than any other, it was supported by the marked favor of the emperor, from Septimius Severus on; in remote areas, it represented all that was visible of Rome's victorious civilization; and when brigands and barbarians descended on the helpless calm of the inner empire, the soldier took on the aura of a deliverer. He led the local defense, he mobilized arms, men, and money. He concentrated civil authority in his hands, at first quite unofficially, but more and more with the sanction of the state. Finally, he and his works were ubiquitous. Four of the preceding chapters [of *Soldier and Civilian*] have been devoted to proving just that, and what they have tried to emphasize is the steadily increasing physical closeness of soldier to civilian. Not only were camps largely abandoned (if they did not turn into cities themselves), but garrisons were fixed in a larger number of cities. On the countryside the *limitaneus* was a common figure, while roads, bridgeheads, and hundreds of miles of frontier received a guard of *burgarii*. In the relatively untroubled and lightly held provinces of Egypt there were, by about A.D. 300, at least sixty different emplacements of troops. Here it must have been hard to get away from army centers, let alone avoid the soldier as trader, as tax collector, judge, policeman, moneylender, farmer, and the soldier forbidden by the Codes simply to "wander."

His influence made its most obvious mark on civilian architecture. Towers, guarded gates, crenelations, moats and so forth, on city walls or on private houses, may be left aside, since they were borrowed only for their usefulness. It is, however, as clear as it is surprising, that early Christian basilicas draw inspiration from camp headquarters buildings. Town plans, too, resembled camps, and within towns, the "Roman-British" forum followed military models. An explanation for such copying is easy to find. Army architects were in constant use throughout the empire, and the emperor who kept them busiest, Hadrian, "brigaded in cohorts, like legionary soldiers, his carpenters, surveyors, architects, and every type of expert in building walls or in decorating" (Aurel. Vict. *Epit.* 14.5).

This quotation hints at the prestige and convenience of military organization, which, by these qualities, put its stamp on other groups quite unconnected with the army. The most striking examples must be looked for in the civil office staffs of the central government, where the lowliest scribbler wore a military belt, was called *miles,* and, after the completion of his *militia, veteranus;* where his superiors were *commentarienses, cornicularii,* and the like—all army ranks—and carried the centurion's swagger stick. But the same sort of imitation can be found also in other branches of government—in the *optiones* and *centuriones* commanding the emperor's freedmen; or even among private guilds. Here officers went by the titles of *principales, centuriones, optiones;* ranks were *centuriae* and *numeri caligatorum;* and members were conducted on "maneuvers." There are religious parallels. Within the body of Mithra's worshippers, "The neophyte, on entering, was bound by an oath *(sacramentum)* like that administered to army recruits, and no doubt also he was branded indelibly, with a hot iron. In the mystical hierarchy, the third grade was 'private' *(miles)*: thereafter the initiate formed part of the holy army of the invincible god." Similar military terminology spread to other pagan worships—of Bacchus, Venus, and Isis; above all, it is found in Christian writers, for whom Christ is *imperator,* bishops *duces,* Christians an *exercitus* or "the legion" of *milites,* the laity *gregarii numeri,* neophytes *tirones,* churches *castra,* and so forth. Outside of any such religious context, metaphors drawn from army procedures perhaps enjoyed a special popularity. Libanius speaks of "the office-holder, who has been posted, as it were, for the defense of the laws, to wage war against their every active enemy"; "of an unusually ambitious person, that he was deserting his *taxis*"; and, in this writer at least, other metaphors of war are especially common.

Soldiers have always had words to lend, technical or slang. Some now current in English, from the Air Force, include "zeroed in" (accurately aimed), "bombed" (drunk), and "tail-spin" (panic); but all languages are full of such borrowings. With Latin and Greek, the problem is more complicated. For one thing, there is the role of the army in teaching Latin to barbarians and Greeks. In areas little Romanized, inscriptions become more often Latin, and better and better Latin, as one approaches a legionary camp, from which radiated the chief forces of Romanization. A very large number of words, with only minor changes, were taken over into Greek, and of these, so far as can be seen from papyri, the greatest number before Diocletian were military: *tribounos,* for example, but scores could be listed. Legions in the East, however, because of more local recruiting, contained men whose first language was Greek, and who knew the language of command not at all, or only in the sketchiest fashion. The transference of the world's capital to Constantinople, the gathering flood of constitutions, orders, quadruplicates, and appeals, and the intention of Constantine and of his successors that all this governing should be carried on in Latin, meant for that language a wider spread. Not only did the terms of the bureaucracy spread, but Constantine specifically prescribed Latin for his armies, and in Egypt it remained in official use for army commanders even to the end of the fifth century. Thus army Latin in the East received a second chance to insinuate itself into Greek.

Among words borrowed by Greek from Roman soldiers occur (besides dozens of good Latin ones) some quite foreign examples: *gaesum* (a kind of spear), *sagos* (a Gallic cloak), *droungos* (a tactical formation), *bandon* (a *vexillum*)—these all Celtic—and others also. Most of these were adopted also by Latin, and rapidly naturalized. *Drungus (hoc est globos, hostium;* Veget. 3.16) is used without any special explanation, in SHA *Probus* 19.2; so Gothic *carrago,* perhaps a kind of cart, in Ammianus 31.7.7 and in SHA *Aurelian* 11.6. This is the process of barbarization in which the army played such a key part. There are also, however, words of a better origin, but distorted by soldiers into some new use: slang or metaphor. A "butterfly" *(papilio)* is a tent, found not only in a handbook of camp planning but also in Tertullian, the Vulgate, and often in the Scriptores Historiae Augustae. *Conterraneus,* "countryman," *hoc castrense verbum* (Plin. *N. H.* praef. 1 D), passed into wider use in vulgar Latin (*TLL* s.v.), and *focaria* ("army wife") appears without comment in the Digest, in inscriptions, and in a legal document of Severan times. Army corruptions like the invented verb *aquor,* "to water" (active, as of horses) or "to go in search of water," are acceptable even to Vergil: *tutis sub moenibus urbis aquantur.*

Literary purists generally looked down their noses at this military influence as so much barbarism. No doubt the kind of Latin spoken in the army was not elegant. Some soldiers—there is no saying how many—could not even write. Against these we may set the poets in uniform: the camp organist at Aquincum writing his wife's epitaph in verse (*CIL* 3.10501), a centurion of Severan times describing how the camp baths at Bu Ngem came to be built, "to refresh the body with swimming," and a cavalryman in Egypt using poetry to adorn the fact that he had completed a five-month term of armed duty (he misspells "month" *meses*). "In the collection of metrical inscriptions, the epitaphs of soldiers form a large and interesting group." There is, too, the third-century centurion who appears on his sarcophagus reading, facing Polyhymnia; around, other men with books; to the rear, *eight* Muses, including one for the theater; and the whole "glorified an 'intellectual household,' given to study in the company of its masters and under the eye of the Muses." Finally, we may add the soldiers of higher rank, though few, who even in the late Empire took an interest in history and philosophy.

Some indirect idea of the level of literacy in the army can be formed from the orations of Hadrian to several African units. He apparently expected to be understood, if not fully appreciated, even in the use of scattered archaisms, rare words, and preciosities, and in a generally careful style. Yet the *allocutio* was a special occasion, and called for an increasingly self-conscious dignity, in speech and setting. It gathered round it connotations of "The Monarch close to His Loyal Troops." Shown in relief on Trajan's and the Antonine columns and on the arches of Septimius Severus and Constantine, it assumed a greater frontality and formality, "definitive and entirely characteristic for late antique art." It inspired the building of special courts, platforms, and halls, in the very middle of camps, and from these seem to have developed significant features—the triapsidal throne room, the Place of Appearance approached through a sort of open-air basilica—essential to Byzantine court ceremonies. But the influence of a military occasion and of military architecture on court ceremonial goes far beyond the *allocutio.*

The emperor's palace in Rome was, from 193, defended by "latticed gates and strong doors" (Dio 74.16.4). "And when [the senators] met [Septimius Severus] at Interamna, they were searched for concealed weapons and only then suffered to greet him as he stood armed in the midst of armed men" (SHA *Sept. Severus* 6.2). His first appearance was typical of the man and of the era to come. Yet he did no more than advance further the transformation of the *princeps* into a pure *imperator,* and of palace into camp *(castra).* Everything to do with the emperor—furniture, pages, treasury, everything—was already called *castrensis,* before Septimius Severus ever entered the scene. By Gallienus's time, the emperor's courtiers bore the name *comitatus,* more strikingly in Greek, *stratopedon.* On coins, the common symbol of a towered gate is perhaps to be interpreted, first, as a *castrum,* and the *castrum* then as "an image of the *Sacrum palatium,* from which emanated the universal authority, wisdom, and military virtue of a divine ruler." These visible proofs of change in the emperor's residence and retinue are of course notorious, and their significance cannot be overemphasized. They represent, in a word, militarization. They belong with the emperor clothed in a general's uniform—even that sedentary septuagenarian, Antoninus Pius—or assuming, as his only concession to peace, the mufti of a Roman soldier, the tunic called a dalmatic, which Commodus (who never in his reign left Italy) wore for a reception of the senate, before going on to the theater. More startling are the garments typical of mere privates, adopted by emperors who wished to declare their yet closer identification with their troops: the "G.I." hood *(caracallus)* which

gave a name to the second Severan, or the *bracae* (breeches) of
Celtic auxiliaries, worn by Julian at his coronation. But then, Julian's
reign initiated the crown-ceremony of the torque and "Schil-
derhebung," the raising of the emperor on a shield. Since his troops
had chosen him, it was only right to incorporate their role formally
into the coronation ceremonies; since he was to assume a position of
emperor-soldier, he was only beginning as he must go on.

Uniforms are loved by the military because they give at once
distinction between ranks and identity within a rank. In Roman civil
society, a particular dress had long been usual and sometimes obligatory for public slaves. It was marked by a transverse band, the
limus; its wearers were called *limocincti.* The toga was forbidden
them. Higher up, senators and equestrians had their separate stripes;
and all wore a toga as opposed to the standard cloak, *caligae,* and
other garments of wartime; but these distinctions, though very important, were not at first elaborated. Only in the third-century army did
regular soldiers assume the red leather *cingulum* and a whitish
chlamys with a purple inset, and whitish trousers, and a tunic with
colored insignia on it. In these articles and in other details of dress
and armor, differences in color, weight, and ornament showed the
various ranks, though whether these differences were fixed and sym-
bolic, or only matters of relative richness, is obscure. A system similar, perhaps less refined, worked well enough in the Middle Ages. It
was Severus Alexander's intention "to assign a peculiar type of clothing to each imperial staff, not only to various ranks—in order that
they might be distinguished by their garments—but also to the slaves
as a class—that they might be easily recognized" (SHA *Severus Alex.*
27.1–2). Though the scheme was scotched for this reign by Paul and
Ulpian, it came to life again in the fourth century as an indirect result
of the militarization of the civil service. Clerks and secretaries re-
tained the uniform of the soldiers from whom they were descended.
Cingulum occurs often as meaning "office," and *discingere* "to discharge from office." Ranks were marked in dress. Yet the most
fundamental distinction lay naturally between civilian (holding no
office at all) and "military," in the late imperial sense (in the armed or
civil service). Those who were not *milites* were strictly ordered to
hold to civilian clothing. Roman senators objected. A compromise
specified togas only for senate meetings. "No senator shall vindicate
for himself the *habitus militaris,* but, leaving aside the terror of the

general's chlamys, put on the garments of peace. . . . Staff members shall also wear civilian cloaks *(paenula),* but shall hold their inner garments closely bound by means of their *cingulum* in such a way, however, that they shall cover their breasts with variegated mantles, and thus by such acknowledgment they shall bear witness to the necessities of their ignoble status." The text shows conveniently the two most important things about uniforms: that they somehow differed by rank, and that the prestige of wearing them was tremendous. They were usurped by private citizens for improper purposes; they permeated government; they reached even to the eunuchs of the court, who "gave themselves airs on the strength of their liveries."

This visible marking of distinctions meant (since the great men of the empire were so commonly active or honorary members of the government) that the aristocracy as such wore uniform. Purple, gold thread, precious stones, and silk were generally reserved for the emperor and his family; the *cingulum,* chlamys, and a certain specified luxury of dress, for his servants, in what has been called "a hierarchy through clothing." One could tell such men in the streets. One addressed them, according to the degree of their importance, by such almost technical terms as *spectabilis, laudabilis, egregius, venerabilis, perfectissimus, sacer,* and *eminentissimus.* In formal assemblies, they were marshaled by costume, title, and, "conformably with military usage, a strict order of advancement by seniority of service." The passion for rank produced, first, a profusion of official positions, each with its appropriate forms of address; then, a division of each, into several classes; finally, a subdivision according to the mode and very hour of promotion.

From their eminence, these government dignitaries surveyed an entire population assigned to ranks. Several social levels were recognized, and were entitled to different treatment before the law— slaves and *coloni, humiliores* and *honestiores.* Every individual was fixed in his spot, except the "sturdy beggar," whom it was a duty to seize and immobilize in the first vacant role that came handy. Armorers, bakers, clerks, doctors, farmers, all had their place, and transmitted it to their heirs, and could not leave for another town, nor take up another occupation, nor even marry freely beyond their appointed boundaries. In practice, considerable movement remained. In theory, the whole population of the empire, as if in an indefinite state of emergency, stood sentinel over some post or function.

This system prevailed certainly by the death of Constantine, however much elaboration it underwent later. Its beginnings have of course been eagerly sought, but in the search, historians are hampered by the dark period before the 290s. It would be safe to say only that development toward universal conscription of Roman society, as it appears in the light of the Codes, was enormously accelerated in the last thirty or forty years of the third century.

What sort of men could it be who would so completely and minutely destroy the freedom of a society? To the conditions of the times, why did that one response seem the natural one, which was actually offered by the later Empire?

Emperors who were the most important historically in the last generation or two of the third century include Aureolus, Gallienus, Claudius, Aurelian, Probus, Carus, Diocletian, Maximian, and Constantius Chlorus. All "of humble birth, and most often uncultivated, the only avenue of success was for them a military one." Their right-hand men, the praetorian prefects, seem to have been without exception men of strictly military background; within their inner council was "a military committee" of *militares;* and they used, as their confidential agents, military police and tribunes, to bind the empire together in a web of espionage. There can be no doubt whatever that the forming influence in the crisis of the later Empire was the military mind.

Over the last four or five centuries, the characteristic behavior of soldiers has suggested very powerfully the effect of army life on ways of thinking. Where one can study it in reasonable detail, there does indeed seem to be a "military mind." It exhibits two loves: of precedent and of rank. As to the first, military training is based on examples from times long past, in procedures long frozen to a set form. It is "by the book," and the principle of seniority tends to place instruction and command in the hands of old men. The army is subject to "outbursts of organizational rigidity which remain baffling to the civilian outsider. Anachronistic survivals are practiced alongside highly effective procedures of military management. Much of the ritualism of the military profession—the constant, minute, and repeated inspection of person and property—are devices which are to be found in any occupation where the risks of personal danger are great. Ritualism is in part a defense against anxiety, but it is also a device for wedding tradition to innovation." Subservience to the past, a dislike of risky change, and a fundamental conservatism mark the soldier.

One can see, too, especially in Prussia, a "hideous spirit of fearful obedience to authority"; but generally, a manner of thinking of people and powers as a ladder. Orders come down from above, obedience is directed upward. There is a fixed place for everyone, and a hierarchy for everything. As late as the eighteenth century, cavalry outranked artillery, and won the honor of the right flank; in the officers' parties of a twentieth-century garrison post, the colonel's lady poured the coffee, because "coffee outranks tea." There is a tendency to see things vertically.

These two loves moved the Roman army. Surely nothing need be said of the love of rank. But to do things by the book was clearly the common practice, too. Military architects give an illustration. Best known are their straight, even roads, and their towers along fortified stretches of the frontiers, at precisely fixed intervals. Some other examples have been mentioned earlier: the standardized house plans in *canabae;* the standardized town walls, in Gaul and Spain; the standardized entranceways, turrets, and the like, in Wales, and (really remarkable) in Africa the line of fortresses, some of which were rebuilt to conform better to a single model. Camp design achieved a specially elaborate, almost ritualistic, uniformity from its general lay-out down to the smallest detail, attested in scores of excavations; but there are the minute instructions of Vegetius (1.21 ff.): the ditch, for instance, is to be dug, "so that it is twelve feet wide and nine feet 'under the line,' as they say (that is, perpendicular)"; and when it is finished, "it is inspected and measured by the centurions, who punish such as have been indolent or negligent." Reminiscent of this are the words of command, unchanged over five or six centuries . . . , and the style of military inscriptions exhibiting "a remarkable consistency throughout the first and second centuries, and in the early third century A.D."; at Corbridge, arms manufacture was carried on in the same way. "The great variety of the weapons, of which each class is clearly standardized within itself, is almost unexpected. It would seem that arrows and darts were classified not only by size and weight, but differently barbed according to the work they had to do." Parade helmets had a specified weight of precious metal on them. And if we turn to an area of activity far removed from these various examples, we find even army worships, the calendar of sacrifices, and the roll of admissable gods regulated on one plan throughout the empire, regardless of local preferences. Soldiers in Dura, in the third century, still celebrated, doubtless with no understanding of what they were doing, the old Italian peasant festivals.

A minute obedience to authorized precedent, and a tendency to reduce men to fixed positions, arranged in a careful hierarchy—these are characteristic of the military mind, Roman or later. Moreover, in the hundred years stretching from roughly A.D. 250 on, it was soldiers who were in a position to form opinion and make changes. It should follow that the characteristic developments of the decline reflect the thought of the Roman army.

This possibility has never been given a fair chance, so to speak. It has been thrust aside by a more popular alternative: the derivation of social, economic, administrative, and constitutional features of the late Empire from the East. To explain such things as state monopolies, hierarchization of society, and even innovations in camp architecture, scholars have ransacked Egypt, Syria, and Persia, from Hellenistic to Sassanian times. At their worst, they have attributed to the men in power, in Rome and Constantinople, such knowledge as one might expect only in some curator of Near Eastern antiquities; but "barrack generals," under pressure of emergency, meeting in great haste the most complex difficulties, surely did not look for help in the vestigial practices of their eastern provinces. They themselves and the agents they trusted came from the North. They knew little that they had not learned in the camp. They had time to act only instinctively, and their instincts were military.

The present study suggests only a tool of explanation. Others may perhaps test its usefulness. The later Empire was to some extent militarized. The emperor, for example, drew closer to his troops, and the balance of power and prestige inclined, under Septimius Severus, towards army officers. So much is generally admitted. The greater part of army influence, in various fields, which has been traced in previous chapters [of *Soldier and Civilian*], has been detected, if not emphasized, by other scholars. What might be tried, however, is a somewhat more confident use of such material to explain wider developments. Take, for illustration, Diocletian's reign, crucial in itself, and occurring in the very middle of our period. Was it, in general character, really a complex of violent changes, or was it as essentially conservative as we might expect from a man of strictly military background? Was Diocletian's reform of taxes modeled on Egyptian and Syrian experiments, or was it, in its basic term *iugatio,* and in its rigid simplicity, just such as a conservative commissary officer might choose? Was his treatment of the civil service radical, or only (for a soldier) logical? Was the further freezing of his subjects in different grades and functions the work of Oriental despotism, or of an impatient commander ignorant of civilian liberties? And did the design of his palace come from the East, or was it not rather created by army architects, using the traditions of Roman castrametation? To these questions, the second answers seem more persuasive.

A. H. M. Jones
THE PRESSURE OF THE BARBARIANS

Why Did the Western Empire Fall?

The causes of the fall of the western empire in the fifth century have been endlessly debated since Augustine's day, but those who have debated the question have all been westerners, and have tended to forget that the eastern empire did not fall until many centuries later. Many of the causes alleged for the fall of the west were common to the east, and therefore cannot be complete and self-sufficient causes. If, as the pagans said in 410, it was the gods, incensed by the apostasy of the empire, who struck it down, why did they not strike down the equally Christian eastern parts? If, as Salvian argues, it was God who sent the barbarians to chastise the sinful Romans, why did He not send barbarians to chastise the equally sinful Constantinopolitans? If Christianity, as Gibbon thought, sapped the empire's morale and weakened it by internal schisms, why did not the more Christian east, with its much more virulent theological disputes, fall first?

We must look then for points in which the two halves of the empire differed. In the first place the western provinces were much more exposed to barbarian attack. The western emperor had to

From *The Decline of the Ancient World,* pp. 362–370, by A. H. M. Jones. Copyright © 1966 by A. H. M. Jones. Reprinted by permission of Longman Group Ltd.

guard the long fronts of the Rhine and the upper Danube, the eastern emperor only the lower Danube. For on the eastern front his neighbor was the Persian empire, a civilized power which was not on the whole aggressive and kept its treaties. If a Persian war broke out, it was a more serious affair than a barbarian invasion, but wars were rare until the sixth century, and they then tested the Roman empire very severely. Moreover, if the western emperor failed to hold any part of the Rhine and Danube fronts, he had no second line of defense; the invaders could penetrate straight into Italy and Gaul, and even into Spain. The eastern emperor, if he failed, as he often did, to hold the lower Danube, only lost control temporarily of the European dioceses; for no enemy could force the Bosphorus and the Hellespont, guarded by Constantinople itself. Asia Minor, Syria and Egypt thus remained sealed off from invasion.

The barbarian invaders soon grasped the strategical position and, even if they first crossed the lower Danube and ravaged Thrace and Illyricum, soon tired of these exhausted lands and, unable to penetrate into the rich lands of Asia Minor, trekked westwards to Italy. This path was successively followed by the Visigoths under Alaric and the Ostrogoths under Theoderic.

In the second place the eastern parts were probably more populous, more intensively cultivated and richer than the western. This is hard to prove and difficult to believe nowadays, when the Balkans, Asia Minor and Syria are poor and thinly peopled, and only Egypt is rich and populous, whereas in the west Italy, France, Britain and the Low Countries are wealthy and densely populated, and only north Africa is poor. But many lines of argument suggest that the reverse was true in Roman times. The population of Egypt was about 8 million, that of Gaul (which included besides modern France the Low Countries and Germany west of the Rhine) can be estimated at about 2½ million. The diocese of Egypt yielded perhaps three times as much revenue as that of Africa. Archaeological evidence proves that many areas now desert or waste in Syria and Asia Minor were inhabited and cultivated in late Roman times, and suggest that much of the most fertile soil in northern Gaul and Britain was still uncleared forest. It is moreover possible to estimate the wealth of different areas in the Roman empire from the number and scale of the public buildings of the cities, since the rich put much of their surplus wealth into such buildings. On this test the Mediterranean lands, eastern and southern Spain, southern Gaul, Italy, Africa, the southern Balkans, Asia Minor, Syria and Egypt were all wealthy, and Asia Minor and Syria the wealthiest of all, whereas Britain, northern Gaul and the Danubian lands were miserably poor. This analysis is borne out by literary testimonies. In the west Sardinia, Sicily and above all Africa, were regarded as the richest provinces, the granaries of the empire, and Aquitania as more fertile than northern Gaul. This implies that the potential fertility of the northern plains had not yet been exploited to the full.

In some other ways the east was superior to the west. It enjoyed much greater political stability and less of its resources were wasted in civil wars. From the accession of Diocletian in 284 to the death of Maurice in 602 there were only five attempted usurpations, those of Domitius Domitianus under Diocletian, of Procopius under Valens, of Basiliscus, Marcian and Leontius under Zeno, and all were quickly subdued without many casualties. In the west there were rebellions or usurpations by Carausius, Maxentius, Alexander, Magnentius, Firmus, Magnus Maximus, Gildo, Constantine, Jovinus and John, most of which involved heavy fighting, and after the death of Valentinian III a succession of ephemeral emperors.

The social and economic structure of the east was healthier than that of the west. In the east more of the land was owned by peasant proprietors, who paid taxes only, and thus a larger proportion of the total yield of agriculture went to the peasantry. In the west a much higher proportion of the land was owned by great landlords, whose tenants had to pay rents in excess of their taxes, and the general condition of the peasantry was therefore poorer. This is reflected in the recurrent revolts of the Bacaudae in Gaul and Spain, which at times contained troops urgently needed elsewhere.

Another result of this difference in social structure was that the landed aristocracy in the west obtained a stranglehold on the administration, with two deleterious results. They were inefficient administrators, and allowed the bureaucracy to add a very appreciable sum to the burden of taxation by their exorbitant fees. They were overindulgent to their own class, and slack in curbing grants of immunity and reductions and remissions of taxes. In the east the administrative machine remained in the hands of men of middle-class origin, who owed their advancement to the imperial government; they kept the expenses of tax collection down to a very reasonable figure, and periodically cancelled reductions of tax granted to landowners. A higher proportion of the total yield of agriculture thus reached the imperial treasury, and less was absorbed by the bureaucracy and by landlords.

Another question may be asked. When the western empire had stood firm for two and a half centuries from the reign of Augustus, and had surmounted the crisis of the mid-third century, and, reorganized by Diocletian, had maintained itself intact for another three generations, why did it so rapidly collapse in the fifth century? Was the collapse primarily due to increased outside pressure or to internal decay or to a mixture of both?

One can only approximately gauge the external pressure on the empire. If one compares two historians who wrote on a similar scale of the first and of the fourth centuries A.D., Tacitus and Ammianus, one gains the impression that in the former period there was no heavy pressure on the frontiers, but in general peace, with only occasional border wars, whereas in the latter the emperors were constantly engaged in checking a breakthrough here and another breakthrough there. The first serious attack on the Roman frontier was under Marcus Aurelius, and in the mid-third century the migrations of the Goths and other East German tribes set up a general movement along the Danube, while the West German tribes grouped in the Frankish and Alamannic federation became more aggressive. The emperors of the late third century managed to restore the line, but it was henceforth held with far more effort than before. In the third quarter of the fourth century the westward movement of the Huns set all the German tribes in motion, and their pressure on the empire was redoubled. The tremendous losses incurred by the western Roman army during this period, amounting it would seem to two-thirds of its effectives, are striking evidence of the severity of the barbarian attacks.

One cause of weakness to the western parts was their administrative separation from the east. Formerly the emperors had been able to draw freely on the wealth of the east to finance the defense of the west. From the time of Diocletian the relatively poor western parts had to make do on their own resources with only occasional aid from the east.

To meet the increased barbarian pressure both halves of the empire enormously increased their armed forces, probably doubling their numbers. How far the high standard of military efficiency established in the principate was kept up, it is difficult to say, but it is unlikely that there was any significant decline. As any reader of Tacitus knows, the army of the early principate was not perfect. In peaceful times discipline became very slack, and the men spent their days on their private avocations and rarely attended a parade. Troops could get out of hand and plunder the provinces they were supposed to protect, and could panic in the face of the enemy. The officers were not professional soldiers and were often incompetent. These and other weaknesses appear in the later Roman empire, but the officers were on the whole of better quality, being experienced professionals. Small bodies of Roman troops still could and did defeat very much larger barbarian hordes in the fourth, fifth and sixth centuries.

The heavy economic burden imposed by the increased size of the army overstrained the resources of the empire and produced a number of weaknesses. It may seem an exaggeration to say that the resources of so large an area as the Roman Empire could be overstrained by feeding, clothing and arming an extra 300,000 men, but it must be remembered that the empire was technologically even more backward than Europe of the Middle Ages. With primitive methods of agriculture, industrial production and transport it took very many more man-hours than today to produce the food for rations, to weave the fabrics for uniforms, to hammer out the arms and armor and to transport all this material by barge and wagon to the frontiers. Taxation had to be enormously increased, and to assess and collect the increased taxes, the civil service had to be expanded, thus increasing the taxation load again.

The heavy burden of taxation was probably the root cause of the economic decline of the empire. Marginal lands, which could not yield a profit to the landlord over and above the taxes, ceased to be cultivated. The population seems also to have shrunk. This is a highly disputable point, but there are distinct signs of a chronic shortage of agricultural manpower, notably the reluctance of landlords to surrender their tenants as recruits, the legislation tying tenants to their farms, the constant attempts of landlords to filch tenants from their neighbors, and the large-scale settlement of barbarians on the land. The shortage was not due to a flight from the land to the towns—the movement was rather in the opposite direction. It was exacerbated by the demands of conscription, but it is difficult to resist the suggestion that the peasant population failed to maintain its numbers. The decline in the cultivated area, though not primarily due to manpower shortage, implies that the rural population did decline. The reason for this was that the peasantry, after paying their taxes, and the tenants their rent, did not retain enough food to rear large families, and many died of malnutrition or of actual starvation in bad seasons or after enemy devastations.

Ideally speaking the empire could of course have reduced the economic burden by rigid efficiency and drastic pruning of superfluities. It maintained large numbers of idle or nominal soldiers and sinecurist civil servants. According to old custom it fed 120,000 citizens of Rome, and added to these 80,000 citizens of Constantinople. These were a direct burden on the treasury. It also tolerated, and indeed encouraged, the growth of other classes of idle mouths, notably the clergy. Paganism had cost very little, its priests, except in Egypt, receiving no remuneration except portions of sacrifices. The churches, with their many thousands of clergy, maintained from agricultural rents and first fruits, constituted a new and substantial burden on the economy. The emperors moreover did nothing to curb the growth of the official aristocracy in numbers and wealth, and thus tolerated and encouraged the increase of another unproductive class.

The basic cause of the economic decline of the empire was in fact the increasing number of (economically speaking) idle mouths—senators with their vast households, decurions, civil servants, lawyers, soldiers, clergy, citizens of the capitals—as compared with the number of producers. The resultant burden of taxation and rents proved too much for the peasantry, who slowly dwindled in numbers.

It has been argued that the empire was weakened by the decay of its trade and industry. It is in fact very doubtful if trade and industry did decay: the production and distribution of high-grade and luxury goods for the rich certainly continued to flourish down to the sixth century, and the bulk of industrial and commercial activity had probably always been devoted to such goods. In any event industry and trade had at all times made so small a contribution to the national income that their decay, if it did occur, was economically unimportant.

This economic pressure was, it must be remembered, as severe in the eastern as in the western parts. The east maintained as large an army and a civil service, and had an even larger and richer body of clergy, if a less wealthy aristocracy, than the west. Its rate of taxation was very high, its marginal lands fell out of cultivation, and its population probably sank. But it had greater reserves of agricultural wealth and manpower on which to draw.

No one who reads the scanty records of the collapse of the western empire can fail to be struck by the apathy of the Roman population from the highest to the lowest. The only instance of concerted self-help by the provincials is the action of the cities of Britain and Armorica in 408, when, failing to receive aid from the usurper Constantine, they organized their own defense against the barbarians, with the subsequent approval of Honorius. In 471–75 Sidonius Apollinaris, the bishop of their city, inspired the Arverni to defend themselves against the Visigoths. In 532 Pudentius raised his province of Tripolitania against the Vandals and, with the aid of a small imperial force, ejected them. In 546 Tullianus, a landlord of Lucania and Bruttium, organized a large body of peasants, which assisted the imperial forces against Totila. These are the only resistance movements of which we know. Elsewhere the upper classes either fled—there is ample evidence for Spain in 409, when the barbarians first broke in, and for the African provinces in 437 and 442, when the Vandals invaded them—or stayed put and collaborated with the barbarian kings. Not that they were active traitors, with one or two notorious exceptions, but they passively accepted their lot. They were very pleased in Africa and Italy when Justinian's armies arrived, but they did very little to help them.

The lower classes were just as inert. Townsmen would generally man the walls, but their object was to avoid a sack, and if guaranteed security they would usually surrender. Peasants, like their betters, sometimes fled in panic, but more often accepted their fate passively. They would fight if given a lead, as by Tullianus, but they would fight on either side. Totila subsequently ordered the landlords under his control to recall their peasants from Tullianus's force, and they meekly obeyed. Later Totila raised his own force of Italian peasants and they fought their fellow-citizens under Tullianus in bloody battles. Among the lower classes again there is very little evidence of active cooperation with the barbarians. In fact only one case is known; in 376 some Thracian miners joined the Goths and guided them to rich villas where stores of food were available. Having recently been recalled to their work from agriculture, they may have had a special grievance. It is alleged by Salvian that some peasants in Gaul fled to the barbarians to escape the oppression of landlords and tax collectors; this is no doubt true, but Salvian is a biased witness and perhaps exaggerates.

This apathy was not peculiar to the western parts; instances of self-help are as rare in the east. Nor was it, so far as we know, anything new. There had been less occasion for civilian resistance to the enemy under the principate, when the armies on the whole held the invaders at the frontier, but no civilian action is recorded when a breakthrough did occur. For many centuries the provincials had been used to being protected by a professional army, and they had indeed, ever since the reign of Augustus, been prohibited by the *lex Iulia de vi* from bearing arms; this law was in force and more or less observed in the fifth century, and Justinian stiffened it by making the manufacture of arms a strict government monopoly. It was only on the rarest occasions that the government appealed to the civil population (including slaves) to take up arms to defend the empire; in 406 when Radagaesus with his horde had broken into Italy, the government appealed for volunteers "for love of peace and country," and in 440, when Gaiseric was threatening to invade Italy, it authorized the provincials to arm themselves to resist Vandal landing parties. It is not known whether either appeal was fruitful; in earlier crises Augustus and Marcus Aurelius had been obliged to apply conscription in Italy.

The general attitude of the provincials to the empire was, and always had been, passive. This is well illustrated under the principate by such panegyrics on the Roman empire as that of Aelius Aristides, and by the provincial cult of Rome and Augustus. Provincials were profoundly grateful to the empire for protecting them from the barbarians and maintaining internal security, and thus enabling them to enjoy and develop the amenities of civilized life in peace. But they felt no active loyalty, no obligation to help the emperor in his task. He was a god, whom they delighted to worship, but who needed no aid from his mortal subjects.

It has been argued that the regimentation of the population into hereditary castes led to inertia and discontent. It is true that many members of the classes affected tried to evade their hereditary obligations, but this does not prove that all were discontented. In any society, however free, most people are content to carry on in their parents' vocation, and it is only an enterprising few who strike out a new line and rise in the social scale. So far as we can tell the enterprising few in the later Roman empire normally succeeded in flouting or evading the law, which was very inefficiently enforced. The extent and the rigidity of the caste system have in any case been exaggerated, and it was, it may be noted, common to both east and west.

There was undoubtedly a decline in public spirit in the later Roman empire, both in the east and in the west. Under the principate there had existed a strong sense of civic patriotism among the gentry, and they had given freely of their time and money not only to improve the amenities of their cities, but to perform many administrative tasks, such as collecting the taxes and levying recruits, delegated to the cities by the imperial government. From the third century onwards this civic patriotism faded, and the imperial government had to rely more and more on its own administrators and civil servants. Under the principate the service of the state had been regarded as a high duty, incumbent on the imperial aristocracy, and on the whole, the government service being small and select, high standards were maintained. Under the later empire the old pagan idea of public service waned and the church taught good Christians to regard the imperial service as dirty work, if not sinful, while the ranks of the administration were greatly expanded and its quality inevitably diluted. Hence the growth of corruption and extortion, leading to popular discontent and waste of the limited resources of the empire. Over a wider field the teaching of the church that salvation was only to be found in the world to come and that the things of this world did not matter may have encouraged apathy and defeatism.

It must however be emphasized that the eastern empire shared to the full these various weaknesses, economic, social and moral, and that it nevertheless survived for centuries as a great power. It was the increasing pressure of the barbarians, concentrated on the weaker western half of the empire, that caused the collapse.

N. H. Baynes
THE DECLINE OF THE ROMAN EMPIRE IN WESTERN EUROPE: SOME MODERN EXPLANATIONS

Norman Hepburn Baynes was born in England in 1877 and educated at Oxford. A specialist in late Roman and Byzantine history, he held the chair of Byzantine History at the University of London. Among his more important writings are The Historia Augusta, Its Date and Purpose, *and* Byzantium, *edited with H. St.-L. B. Moss. His best known work is the masterly survey,* The Byzantine Empire.

It is the purpose of this paper to consider a few of the more outstanding contributions towards the solution of this familiar problem propounded since the publication in 1898 of Sir Samuel Dill's book on *Roman Society in the last century of the Western Empire* (2nd ed., 1899). It may well appear somewhat surprising that I should venture to speak on such a topic, since my own work, such as it is, has been concerned rather with the history of the Byzantine Empire. And yet for a student of Byzantine history the problem has a special interest: he is forced to consider that problem not merely as a West European issue, but rather to compare and contrast the historical development in the western and eastern provinces of the Empire. He is compelled to raise the question: Why was it that the Roman Empire failed to survive in Western Europe while it endured for a further millennium in the East? The very fact that he is primarily interested in the history of the Byzantine Empire enables him to approach the Western problem from a different angle and to treat that problem in a wider setting and not in isolation. That is my apologia for what might otherwise appear to be an inexcusable impertinence. In a word I desire to ask what general considerations can be adduced to explain the fact, that in Western Europe there is a cultural break—a caesura—while in the East Roman world the cultural development is continuous, the Hellenistic and Roman traditions being gradually fused to form the civilization of the Byzantine Empire.

Of the recent explanations of the decline of the Roman power in

Reprinted from the *Journal of Roman Studies* 33 (1943): 29–35, by permission of the Society for the Promotion of Roman Studies.

Western Europe we may first take that of Vladimir G. Simkhovitch who in the *Political Science Quarterly* for 1916 published an article under the title "Rome's Fall Reconsidered" in which he attributed the collapse of the Roman power to the exhaustion of the soil of Italy and of the provinces. That article has been reprinted—somewhat incongruously—in the author's book *Towards the Understanding of Jesus.* The evil began under the Republic: in Cato's time agriculture had already declined in the greater part of Italy. When asked what is the most profitable thing in the management of one's estate he replied "Good pasturage." What is the next best? "Fairly good pasturage." What is the third best? "Bad pasturage." And the fourth best? "Arare"—agriculture. Simkhovitch admits that the Romans possessed great agricultural knowledge. "All that is implied by the agricultural revolution," he writes, "the seeding of grasses and legumes, the rotation of crops, yes even green manuring, all that was perfectly known to the Romans. Why was it not practiced for two thousand years or more? I do not know." Columella was already drawing upon a literary tradition in his counsel to farmers: his mistakes prove that he had never witnessed the operations which he describes. To seed alfalfa one cyathus for 50 square feet, which amounts to several bushels per acre, is an impossible proposition. Province after province was turned by Rome into a desert: draining was neglected, and deserted fields became mosquito- and malaria-infested swamps. The "inner decay" of the Roman Empire in all its manifold manifestations was in the last analysis entirely based upon the endless stretches of barren, sterile, and abandoned fields in Italy and the provinces. The evidence adduced by Simkhovitch is drawn for the most part from writers of the Republic or of the period of the early Principate, but from the Christian Empire he quotes Constantine's legislation in favor of the children of the poor who have not the means to provide for their offspring, and also the constitution of Valentinian, Arcadius and Theodosius giving permission to the squatter to cultivate deserted fields. Against those who would maintain that the flight from the land was caused by oppressive taxation he contends that it was precisely the exhaustion of the soil which rendered the burden of taxation oppressive: it was because so much land was uncultivated that taxation pressed so heavily upon those who still continued the farming of their fields. The limits which confine the productivity of man's labor become for society physical conditions of existence from which it cannot escape. It was these limits set by the exhaustion of the soil which rendered the doom of Rome inevitable.

There is no doubt truth in this picture of the decline of agriculture: for the later Empire it may well be an accurate description of some parts of Italy: in A.D. 395 the abandoned fields of Campania alone amounted to something over 528,000 *jugera;* but in itself it is inadequate as an explanation of the fall of Rome. For in one country at least—Egypt—there can be no question of soil-exhaustion, and it is precisely from Egypt that we have our earliest reports of the flight from the land, of the disappearance of villages through depopulation. Modern studies of economic conditions in Egypt have demonstrated the fatal effects of the methods of administrative exploitation employed by the Roman government in that province. The burden of taxation here certainly came first, and the decay of agriculture was its result and not its cause. Further, the sweeping generalizations of Simkhovitch's paper cannot be sustained: even in the fifth century of our era where a resident proprietor supervised the cultivation of his own estate there can be no question of soil-exhaustion. Read again Ausonius's poem of his expedition in the valley of the Moselle, read the letters of Sidonius Apollinaris: still in the Gaul of the fifth century it is clear that they were smiling fields and well-cultivated farms. The real danger of the *latifundia* lay, I am convinced, in the fact that they were for the most part managed by bailiffs for owners who were absentee landlords, men who drew money from their estates in order to spend it in Rome, Ravenna, or some provincial capital. The primary cause of the agricultural decline is to be found in the abuses of the fiscal system, in the scourge of corporate responsibility for the collection of the taxes which ruined the municipal aristocracy of the city *curiae,* and perhaps above all in the absence of the personal supervision of the proprietor and the unprincipled use of authority by irresponsible bailiffs, controlling the cultivation of the large estates which now absorbed so great a part of the land of the empire. Soil-exhaustion is, in fact, an inadequate explanation of the collapse of the Roman power.

Another theory has been proposed by Professor Ellsworth Huntington—that of climatic change. The great sequoias of California—the big trees of a familiar advertisement—have been growing for some three or even four thousand years. Each year in the trunk of the tree there is clearly marked the circle of the year's growth: when the tree is felled these rings can be traced and according to their width a chronological chart of climatic variation can be established: the years of considerable width of ring recording the effect of favorable climatic conditions, the narrower rings marking the result of less favorable climate. In this way for the area of the sequoias the variations in climate can be traced for at least 3,000 years. On this basis Ellsworth Huntington constructed his theory. In an article published in 1917 in the *Quarterly Journal of Economics* on "Climatic Change and Agricultural Exhaustion as Elements in the Fall of Rome" he suggested that the climate of the Mediterranean world and that of California have always undergone similar modifications: that from the chronological chart of Californian climate one is accordingly entitled to reconstruct the changes in the climate of the Mediterranean area during the course of the history of Rome, and from the record of such changes we may conclude that the fall of Rome was due to a decline in the rainfall from which the Mediterranean world suffered during the fourth, fifth, and sixth centuries of our era. It is easy to object that on Professor Huntington's own showing the latter part of the second century and the first half of the third century marked a climatic improvement: it might be hard to trace any corresponding increase in prosperity in the history of the Empire during this period. But a more serious objection would point to the hazardous character of the fundamental assumption. Records of rainfall in the neighborhood of the great trees have only been kept for about half a century; Professor Huntington prints a table of four year-groups in order to establish the climatic parallelism between California and the Mediterranean area (*Quarterly Journal of Economics* xxxi, 1916–17, 193):

    I. Seven years of heaviest rainfall in California
    II. Eighteen years with heavy rainfall in California
    III. Seventeen years with light rainfall in California
    IV. Thirteen years with least rainfall in California

The table presents the following figures:

	San Francisco	Rome	Naples
I.	8.3 in.	10.7 in.	11.5 in.
II.	4.5 in.	10.6 in.	11.0 in.
III.	3.4 in.	9.8 in.	9.2 in.
IV.	1.9 in.	9.6 in.	8.6 in.

"The columns vary," writes Professor Huntington, "in harmony with the California rainfall." That is true, but the disparity in the amount of the decline in rainfall between California and Rome—in California a fall from 8.3 in. to 1.9 in., in Rome a fall only from 10.7 in. to 9.6 in.—is very striking, and it is not easy to see what conclusions can justifiably be drawn from such figures.

But that is not all: the matter does not remain as it stood in 1917. In 1925 the Carnegie Institute of Washington published further discussion of the Big Tree as a climatic measure, and it now appears uncertain what part is played respectively by temperature and what by rainfall in the yearly growth. Thus a further element of ambiguity is introduced into the problem. Before this Ossa of doubt piled upon a Pelion of uncertainty the confidence of a mere student of history may well quail, and for the present I should hesitate to call in aid Nature's yardstick as a solution of our historical perplexities. The great trees still keep their climatic secret.

From Nature we may turn to the human factor in our search for the causes of the collapse of the Roman power. Otto Seeck has, I think, found no followers in his attempt to charge the third-century Roman emperors with the responsibility for that collapse. Through their continued *Ausrottung der Besten*—the persistent extermination of capacity and individual merit—the Caesars bred a terror of distinction and encouraged the spread of that slave mentality which issued logically and naturally in the triumph of Christianity—the Beggars' Religion—*die Religion des Betteltums.* An inverted Darwinism stamped out originality from the Empire: no man remained with the courage to be the master of his fate—the captain of his own soul. The way was open for "Byzantinismus," for crawling servility and fawning adulation of authority. Here the prejudice of one who was inspired by a passionate and life-long hatred of the Christian faith has, I cannot but feel, attempted to wrest history to its own purpose. Is there indeed any single century in the annals of the Empire which can show so many men of outstanding personality as can the fourth century of our era? Surely Professor Lot is not far from the truth when he exclaims: "If ever there were supermen in human history they are to be found in the Roman emperors of the third and fourth centuries"—men who shouldered the burden of a tottering world and resolutely refused to despair of the Republic. And beside the Roman emperors stand in the Christian camp such figures as Athansius and

S. Basil in the East, as Ambrose and Augustine in the West. There is little of crawling servility in such men as these. The wonder of the fourth century to my mind is rather the heroic courage and the desperate resolution with which men strove to preserve that imperial organization which alone safeguarded the legacy of the ancient world. Further, you will not have failed to notice with what rigor Seeck presses the theory of the hereditary transmissibility of ἀρετή. So thoroughgoing a conviction might well rejoice the heart of a champion of an unreformed House of Lords. No, *Die Ausrottung der Besten* will not suffice to explain the decline of the Roman power.

Professor Tenney Frank, of the Johns Hopkins University, Baltimore, has approached the problem from another angle. From an elaborate statistical study of the Corpus of Latin inscriptions he concludes that Rome and the Latin West were flooded by an invasion of Greek and Oriental slaves: as these were emancipated and thus secured Roman citizenship the whole character of the citizen body was changed; on the basis of a consideration of some 13,900 sepulchral inscriptions he argues that nearly 90 percent of the Roman-born inhabitants of the Western capital were of foreign extraction. What lay behind and constantly reacted on those economic factors which have generally been adduced to explain the decline of the Roman power was the fact that those who had built Rome had given way to a different race. "The whole of Italy as well as the Romanized portions of Gaul and Spain were during the Empire dominated in blood by the East." In this fact Tenney Frank would find an explanation of the development from the Principate to the Dominate—the triumph of absolutism, of the spread of Oriental religions, the decline in Latin literature and the growing failure in that gift for the government of men which had built up the Empire.

But the foundations on which this far-reaching theory rests are not above suspicion. The nationality of Roman slaves is but rarely expressly stated in the sepulchral inscriptions, and thus it is upon the appearance of a Greek name for slave or freedman that Tenney Frank has inferred an Oriental origin. The legitimacy of this inference has been questioned by Miss Mary Gordon in her able study of the "Nationality of Slaves under the early Roman Empire," *JRS* xiv, 1924. A slave was a personal chattel, and slave-dealer or slave-owner could give to the slave any name which in his unfettered choice he might select: the slave dealers with whom Romans first came in contact were Greeks and thus, as Miss Gordon says, "Greek was the original language of the slave trade and this is reflected in servile nomenclature much as the use of French on modern menus and in the names affected by dressmakers suggests the history and associations of particular trades." In fact the nomenclature of the slave in the ancient world was scarcely less arbitrary than are the modern names given to our houses, our puddings, our horses or our dogs. An attempt to determine the domicile of origin of our cats or dogs solely by the names which their owners have given them would hardly be likely to produce results of high scientific value. The outlandish names of barbarian captives reduced to slavery would naturally be changed to more familiar forms, and Latin nomenclature was singularly poor and unimaginative: the Greek names were well known and resort to these was easy. It may be said that this reasoning is largely *a priori* and of little cogency. But Ettore Cicotti in a recent paper on "Motivi demografici e biologici nella rovina della civiltà antica" in *Nuova Rivista storica,* Anno xiv, fasc. i–ii, has adduced an interesting historical parallel. L. Livi (*La schiavitù domestica nei tempi di mezzo e nei moderni, Ricerche storiche di un antropologo,* Roma, 1928) in 1928 published documents which his father copied from the State Archives of Florence. These documents record 357 sales of slaves: the transactions date from the years 1366 to 1390— for the most part from the years 1366 to 1370. The majority of the slaves were of Tartar origin, though some were Greeks, Rumanians, etc. In these records the slave's original name is generally given and then follows the Italian name by which the slave is known. Thus the name of Lucia occurs forty-two times and represents such original names as Marchecta, Gingona, Erina, Minglacha, Saragosa, Casabai, Alterona and many others. Similarly the name of Caterina is given to slaves of Greek, Tartar, Turkish, Circassian, and Russian origin and has taken the place of such barbarous names as Coraghessan, Chrittias, Colcatalo, Tagaton, and Melich. The parallel is very instructive.

But this is not all: the sepulchral inscriptions studied by Tenney Frank extend over a period of three centuries: suppose that Rome had during the early Empire a population of some 800,000 with an annual mortality of 20 percent: in those three centuries the deaths would number 4.8 million. Tenney Frank has examined 13,900 inscriptions and those are derived from imperial and aristocratic *columbaria:* here the slaves would be better off and the percentage of accomplished foreign slaves would be higher: what of the nameless dead whom no record preserved, whose bodies lay in the vast common burial pits of the slave proletariat? These 13,900 dead who left permanent memorials behind them cannot be regarded as really representative of the general servile population of the city: we are not justified in using the percentage obtained from these records and applying it as though it were applicable to the whole class of slaves and of freedmen.

In the light of this criticism Tenney Frank's statistics are vitiated, and it must be admitted that the nationality of the slaves of Rome under the early Empire remains a matter of conjecture. There must have been a far greater number derived from Western Europe than are allowed for on Tenney Frank's calculations.

A somewhat different form of biological explanation is given by Professor Nilsson in his well-known book *Imperial Rome.* The most important problem for the Empire was that of race: that was decisive, for upon it depended the quality of Roman civilization. Culture rests on racial character. If the alien races and barbarian peoples were to be assimilated, they must be inter-penetrated by their conquerors. Since the Roman world was of vast extent and those of alien race were very numerous, an increase in the birth-rate of the Romans was required: instead of this the Roman birth-rate declined: the blood of the Romans became more and more diluted, and in place of the Romanization of the Empire a civilization of intercommunication and intercourse resulted in a mingling of races—an unchecked "mongrelization." Under the Empire cross-breeding, hybridization, spread throughout the provinces and in this widespread realm of mongrels all stable spiritual and moral standards were lost.

I confess that as soon as the word "race" is introduced into any discussion i realize that my only safe course lies in a resolute silence, for I have never been able to understand the precise significance of that ambiguous term. But when folk begin to ascribe all kinds of moral and spiritual failings to race-mixture it will hardly be expected that an Englishman will accept the insinuation without a protest. It is beyond calculation to estimate how many races and peoples have gone to his ethnological make-up, and he will not readily admit that the results of "mongrelization" have in his case been wholly deplorable. As an Englishman I am unlikely to discuss dispassionately the theory of Professor Nilsson. And unfortunately I am also a student of

Byzantine history and as such I am convinced that the essential condition of the prosperity of the later Roman Empire was its possession of Asia Minor—that reservoir alike of money and of men. And Asia Minor of the Byzantines was surely man's most stupendous effort in race-mixture to which history can point: it was an ethnological museum. Professor Nilsson, to be quite frank, will have his work cut out to persuade an English Byzantinist that race-mixture is of necessity so poisonous and deadly a process. I had better leave it at that: you had best form your own judgment on the theory without further comment from me.

There still remains, however, the explanation of Professor Rostovtzeff as set forth in his *Social and Economic History of the Roman Empire*, a masterpiece for which any student of imperial Rome must have a sincere admiration. Professor Rostovtzeff's explanation of the collapse of the Roman power can be briefly summarized. It was through the medium of the *municipia*—of the towns—that Rome had unified Italy, and when she extended her conquests into the West of Europe she naturally favored the growths of towns as centers of Romanization. But the towns drew their wealth from the countryside, and the peasants bitterly resented this exploitation of their own class by the *bourgeoisie*. Under the peace of the Empire the civilian population became unfitted for the life of the military camps, and it was from the rude vigor of the peasantry that in the crisis of the third century the Roman armies were recruited. The peasant of the army made common cause with the peasant of the countryside and both waged a war of extermination against their oppressors of the city. The explanation of the downfall of the aristocracy and with them of the ancient civilization is thus to be found in a class-conscious alliance between the soldier and the worker on the land. Professor Rostovtzeff, it must be remembered, has seen in his native country an aristocratic regime overthrown by a similar alliance. And the only answer to this theory that I can give is quite simply that I can find no support for it in our extant sources. I have consulted every reference to the authorities cited by Professor Rostovtzeff and in my judgment none of them supports his reading of the facts. So far as I can see the constant terror of the peasants is the soldier: the last menace to a defaulting debtor is (according to the papyri) the creditor's threat: "I will send a soldier after you." The soldier is to the peasant what Napoleon or the policeman has been to successive generations of children in English nurseries. To the Roman peasant and soldier of the third century of our era there had not been granted a revelation of the gospel according to Karl Marx.

And thus I come back as a student of Byzantine history to the difficulty to which I referred at the beginning of this lecture. I believe that there was in Western Europe a break in the cultural development and that there was no corresponding break in the development of civilization in the Eastern provinces of the Roman Empire. To a Byzantinist, therefore, the problem which we are considering necessarily assumes a dual aspect: what he must discover, if he is to gain any intellectual satisfaction from the inquiry, is precisely the *differentia* which distinguishes the history of the Western provinces from that of the *partes orientales.* And so many of the modern explanations do not provide him with any such *differentia.* "Die Ausrottung der Besten," civil wars, and imperial jealousy of outstanding merit did not affect the West alone: the whole Roman world suffered from these scourges: the brutality of an undisciplined soldiery was likewise an evil common to both halves of the Empire. Soil-exhaustion, climatic change, these must have affected the entire Mediterranean area. The oppression of civil servants, the decay of the municipal senates, the flight from the land—all these ills the Eastern provinces were not spared. Greeks and Orientals invaded the West and we are told caused the collapse of the Roman power there; but in the East these same Greeks and Orientals sustained the Empire against unceasing assaults for another millennium: it seems mysterious. And therefore in closing it only remains for me to state the *differentia* as I see it and to suggest an explanation of this diversity in the history of East and West—an explanation which is so humiliatingly simple that I am constrained to believe that it must be right.

You realize then that I speak as a student of Byzantine history: a Byzantinist looks at the world of Western Europe. As I conceive of it, culture is essentially a social thing: it is born of intercourse and it needs a conscious solidarity of interest in order to sustain it. Roman civilization depended upon intercommunication, upon the influences radiating from the capital and returning to the capital for reinforcement. Such free communication, however, can be preserved only within an area which is safeguarded from violence: the Roman Empire was such an area safeguarded by the civil administration and by the frontier screen of the military forces. The civil service and the army together formed the steel framework which maintained the entire structure of civilization. It is perhaps with the Emperor Hadrian that one first observes a conscious realization of this function of the Roman power. The area of civilization is delimited on permanent lines: not expansion of territory, but concentration of resources in order to protect the solidarity of culture—that is the emperor's task. The barbarian invasions broke into this area of intercourse, and the establishment of barbarian kingdoms on Roman soil destroyed the single administration which was its counterpart. And the fatal significance of the establishment of these barbarian kingdoms lay in the fact that they withdrew from the Empire not only Roman soil, but also the revenues derived therefrom. Africa lost to the Vandals, Spain occupied by Sueve and Alan and Visigoth: Southern France a Visigothic kingdom and the rest of Gaul a battleground on which Aëtius fought and fought again: Italy alone remained as a source of revenue, and Italy was an impoverished land. The Western state was bankrupt. And the defense of the Empire demanded money, for Rome had so effectually provided the area of peaceful intercourse in Western Europe that her subjects were no longer soldiers: if battles were to be won they must be fought by barbarian mercenaries and for mercenaries to fight they must be paid. Further, Rome's effort in the West was a struggle with a double front: against the barbarian on land and against the Vandal fleet upon the sea. Rome possessed no technical superiority such as the invention of gunpowder might have given her, such as later the secret for the composition of the "Greek fire" gave to the Byzantine navy. Thus the tragedy of the Empire in the West lay precisely in the fact that she had not the wherewithal to keep at one and at the same time a mercenary army in the field and a fleet in commission. And the *differentia* which distinguishes the situation in the East of the Empire is in my judgment that, while the Danubian provinces were continuously ravaged, Asia Minor was for the most part untroubled by invasions: Asia Minor remained as I have said a reservoir alike of men and money. It was this reservoir which the West lacked. The West could throw no counterpoise into the scale against the supremacy of the barbarian; but the East amongst its own subjects numbered the hardy mountaineers—the Isaurians— and the fellow-countrymen of the Isaurian Tarasicodissa, whom history knows as the Emperor Zeno, could meet the menace of the barbarian mercenary and when the supremacy of the Alan Aspar had been broken, the Empire could send the Isaurian back to his mountains and Anastasius, an aged civilian who had only just escaped consecration as a bishop, could rule unchallenged. And as a consequence of the triumph of the civil power, the civil administration—the steel framework which maintained Byzantine civilization—was likewise preserved, and from the city of Constantine culture radiated and through intercourse with the capital was again reinforced. Here is preserved that conscious solidarity in the maintenance of civilization which guaranteed a real continuity. In the West there are survivals from the ancient world—true—a branch lopped from a tree may still produce shoots; but for all that the continuity of life is broken: the doom of decay is sure. Gregory of Tours is a remarkable man, but he is a lonely figure and he feels himself isolated. And against that figure I would set a scene at a Byzantine court—when the Emperor's barbarian mistress appeared in her radiant beauty at a reception, one courtier uttered the words οὐ νέμεσις: the barbarian queen did not understand the allusion, but for Byzantines the two words were enough to summon up the picture of Helen as she stood before the greybeards on the walls of Troy. So well did the aristocracy of East Rome know their Homer: such is the solidarity of Byzantine culture. In a word it was the pitiful poverty of Western Rome which crippled her in her effort to maintain that civil and military system which was the presupposition for the continued life of the ancient civilization.

III NOT DECLINE BUT TRANSFORMATION

Peter Brown
GEOGRAPHICAL TRANSFORMATION

Peter Brown was born in Dublin in 1935. He received his MA at New College, Oxford, and was a Harmsworth Senior Scholar at Merton College, Oxford, a Prize Fellow at All Souls College, Oxford, a Junior Research Fellow, a Senior Research Fellow, and a Fellow at All Souls College. He was also a Lecturer in Medieval History at Merton College, Oxford, a Special Lecturer in late Roman and early Byzantine History, and a Reader at the University of Oxford. His publications include Augustine of Hippo, The World of Late Antiquity, *and* Religion and Society in the Age of St. Augustine.

This book [*The World of Late Antiquity*] is a study of social and cultural change. I hope that the reader will put it down with some idea of how, and even of why, the Late Antique world (in the period from about A.D. 200 to about 700) came to differ from "classical" civilization, and of how the headlong changes of this period, in turn, determined the varying evolution of western Europe, of eastern Europe and of the Near East.

To study such a period one must be constantly aware of the tension between change and continuity in the exceptionally ancient and well-rooted world around the Mediterranean. On the one hand, this is notoriously the time when certain ancient institutions, whose absence would have seemed quite unimaginable to a man of about A.D. 250, irrevocably disappeared. By 476, the Roman Empire had vanished from western Europe; by 655, the Persian Empire had vanished from the Near East. It is only too easy to write about the Late Antique world as if it were merely a melancholy tale of "Decline and Fall": of the end of the Roman Empire as viewed from the West; of the Persian, Sassanian empire, as viewed from Iran. On the other hand, we are increasingly aware of the astounding new beginnings associated with this period: we go to it to discover why Europe became Christian and why the Near East became Muslim; we have become extremely sensitive to the "contemporary" quality of the new, abstract art of this age; the writings of men like Plotinus and Augustine surprise us, as we catch strains—as in some unaccus-

From *The World of Late Antiquity*, pp. 7–21, by Peter Brown, copyright © 1971 by Thames and Hudson Ltd., London. Reprinted by permission of Harcourt Brace Jovanovich, Inc.

tomed overture—of so much that a sensitive European has come to regard as most "modern" and valuable in his own culture.

Looking at the Late Antique world, we are caught between the regretful contemplation of ancient ruins and the excited acclamation of new growth. What we often lack is a sense of what it was like to live in that world. Like many contemporaries of the changes we shall read about, we become either extreme conservatives or hysterical radicals. A Roman senator could write as if he still lived in the days of Augustus, and wake up, as many did at the end of the fifth century A.D., to realize that there was no longer a Roman emperor in Italy. Again, a Christian bishop might welcome the disasters of the barbarian invasions, as if they had turned men irrevocably from earthly civilization to the Heavenly Jerusalem, yet he will do this in a Latin or a Greek unselfconsciously modeled on the ancient classics; and he will betray attitudes to the universe, prejudices and patterns of behavior that mark him out as a man still firmly rooted in eight hundred years of Mediterranean life.

How to draw on a great past without smothering change. How to change without losing one's roots. Above all, what to do with the stranger in one's midst—with men excluded in a traditionally aristocratic society, with thoughts denied expression by a traditional culture, with needs not articulated in conventional religion, with the utter foreigner from across the frontier. These are the problems which every civilized society has had to face. They were particularly insistent in the Late Antique period. I do not imagine that a reader can be so untouched by the idea of classical Greece and Rome or so indifferent to the influence of Christianity, as not to wish to come to some judgment on the Late Antique world that saw the radical transformation of the one and the victory over classical paganism of the other. But I should make it plain that, in presenting the evidence, I have concentrated on the manner in which the men of the Late Antique world faced the problem of change.

The Roman Empire covered a vast and diverse territory: the changes it experienced in this period were complex and various. They range from obvious and well-documented developments, such as the repercussions of war and high taxation on the society of the third and fourth centuries, to shifts as intimate and mysterious as those that affected men's relations to their own body and to their immediate neighbors. I trust that the reader will bear with me, therefore, if I begin the first part of this book with three chapters that sketch out the changes in the public life of the empire, from A.D. 200 to 400, and then retrace my steps to analyze those less public, but equally decisive, changes in religious attitudes that took place over the same period. I have done my best to indicate where I consider that changes in the social and economic conditions of the empire intermingled with the religious developments of the age.

Throughout this period, the Mediterranean and Mesopotamia are the main theaters of change. The world of the northern barbarians remained peripheral to these areas. Britain, northern Gaul, the Danubian provinces after the Slav invasions of the late sixth century fall outside my purview. The narrative itself gravitates towards the eastern Mediterranean; the account ends more naturally at the Baghdad of Harun al-Rashid than at the remote Aachen of his contemporary, Charlemagne. I trust that the reader (and especially the medievalist who is accustomed to surveys that concentrate on the emergence of a post-Roman western society) will forgive me if I keep to this area. For western Europe, he will have those sure guides, to whom we are both equally indebted.

No one can deny the close links between the social and the spiritual revolution of the Late Antique period. Yet, just because they are so intimate, such links cannot be reduced to a superficial relationship of "cause and effect." Often, the historian can only say that certain changes coincided in such a way that the one cannot be understood without reference to the other. A history of the Late Antique world that is all emperors and barbarians, soldiers, landlords and tax-collectors would give as colorless and as unreal a picture of the quality of the age, as would an account devoted only to the sheltered souls, to the monks, the mystics, and the awesome theologians of that time. I must leave it to the reader to decide whether my account helps him to understand why so many changes, of such different kinds, converged to produce that very distinctive period of European civilization—the Late Antique world.

The Boundaries of the Classical World: c. A.D. 200

"We live round a sea," Socrates had told his Athenian friends, "like frogs round a pond." Seven hundred years later, in A.D. 200, the classical world remained clustered round its "pond": it still clung to the shores of the Mediterranean. The centers of modern Europe lie far to the north and to the west of the world of ancient men. To travel to the Rhineland, for them, was to go "half-way to the barbarians": one typical southerner even took his dead wife all the way back home, from Trier to Pavia, to bury her safely with her ancestors! A Greek senator from Asia Minor, posted to a governorship on the Danube, could only pity himself: "The inhabitants . . . lead the most miserable existence of all mankind," he wrote, "for they cultivate no olives and they drink no wine."

The Roman Empire had been extended as far as had seemed necessary at the time of the republic and the early empire, to protect and enrich the classical world that had already existed for centuries round the coast of the Mediterranean. It is the extraordinary tide of Mediterranean life that strikes us about this empire at its apogee in the second century A.D. This tide had washed further inland than ever previously; in North Africa and the Near East, it would never reach as far again. For a short time, an officers' mess modeled on an Italian country-villa faced the Grampians in Scotland. A checkerboard town, with amphitheater, library and statues of classical philosophers looked out over the Hodna range, at Timgad, in what are now the bleak southern territories of Algeria. At Dura-Europos, on the Euphrates, a garrison-town observed the same calendar of public festivals as at Rome. The Late Antique world inherited this amazing legacy. One of the main problems of the period from 200 to 700 was how to maintain, throughout a vast empire, a style of life and a culture based originally on a slender coastline studded with classical city-states.

In the first place, the classical Mediterranean had always been a world on the edge of starvation. For the Mediterranean is a sea surrounded by mountain ranges: its fertile plains and river-valleys are like pieces of lace sewn on to sackcloth. Many of the greatest cities of classical times were placed within sight of forbidding highlands. Every year their inhabitants ransacked the surrounding countryside to feed themselves. Describing the symptoms of widespread malnutrition in the countryside in the middle of the second century, the doctor Galen observed:

The city-dwellers, as was their practice, collected and stored enough corn for all the coming year immediately after the harvest. They carried off all

*the wheat, the barley, the beans and the lentils and left what remained to
the countryfolk.*

Seen in this light, the history of the Roman Empire is the history of
the ways in which 10 percent of the population, who lived in the
towns and have left their mark on the course of European civilization,
fed themselves, in the summary manner described by Galen, from the
labors of the remaining 90 percent who worked the land.

Food was the most precious commodity in the ancient Mediterranean. Food involved transport. Very few of the great cities of the
Roman Empire could hope to supply their own needs from their
immediate environment. Rome had long depended on the annual
sailing of the grain-fleet from Africa: by the sixth century A.D., Constantinople drew 175,200 tons of wheat a year from Egypt.

Water is to all primitive systems of transport what railways have
been in modern times: the one, indispensable artery for heavy freight.
Once a cargo left the waters of the Mediterranean or of a great river,
its brisk and inexpensive progress changed to a ruinous slow-motion.
It cost less to bring a cargo of grain from one end of the Mediterranean to another than to carry it another seventy-five miles inland.

So the Roman Empire always consisted of two, overlapping
worlds. Up to A.D. 700, great towns by the sea remained close to each
other: twenty days of clear sailing would take the traveler from one
end of the Mediterranean, the core of the Roman world, to the other.
Inland, however, Roman life had always tended to coagulate in little
oases, like drops of water on a drying surface. The Romans are
renowned for the roads that ran through their empire: but the roads
passed through towns where the inhabitants gained all that they ate,
and most of what they used, from within a radius of only thirty miles.

It was inland, therefore, that the heavy cost of empire was most
obvious, along the verges of the great land routes. The Roman Empire appears at its most cumbersome and brutal in the ceaseless
effort it made to hold itself together. Soldiers, administrators,
couriers, their supplies, had to be constantly on the move from
province to province. Seen by the emperors in 200, the Roman world
had become a cobweb of roads, marked by the staging-posts at
which each little community would have to assemble ever-increasing
levies of food, clothing, animals and manpower to support the court
and the army.

As for those who served the needs of this rough machine, such compulsions were, at least, nothing new. In places, they were as old as civilization itself. In Palestine, for instance, Christ had warned his hearers how to behave when an official should "requisition you to walk with him (carrying his baggage) for a mile." Even the word the Evangelist used for "requisition" was not, originally, a Greek word: it derived from the Persian, it dated back over five hundred years, to the days when the Achaemenids had stocked the famous roads of their vast empire by the same rough methods.

Yet the Roman Empire, that had sprawled so dangerously far from the Mediterranean by 200, was held together by the illusion that it was still a very small world. Seldom has a state been so dependent on so delicate a sleight of hand. By 200, the empire was ruled by an aristocracy of amazingly uniform culture, taste and language. In the West, the senatorial class had remained a tenacious and absorptive elite that dominated Italy, Africa, the Midi of France and the valleys of the Ebro and the Guadalquivir; in the East, all culture and all local power had remained concentrated in the hands of the proud oligarchies of the Greek cities. Throughout the Greek world no difference in vocabulary or pronunciation would betray the birthplace of any well-educated speaker. In the West, bilingual aristocrats passed unselfconsciously from Latin to Greek; an African landowner, for instance, found himself quite at home in a literary *salon* of well-to-do Greeks at Smyrna.

Such astonishing uniformity, however, was maintained by men who felt obscurely that their classical culture existed to exclude alternatives to their own world. Like many cosmopolitan aristocracies—like the dynasts of late feudal Europe or the aristocrats of the Austro-Hungarian Empire—men of the same class and culture, in any part of the Roman world, found themselves far closer to each other than to the vast majority of their neighbors, the "underdeveloped" peasantry on their doorstep. The existence of the "barbarian" exerted a silent, unremitting pressure on the culture of the Roman Empire. The "barbarian" was not only the primitive warrior from across the frontier: by 200, this "barbarian" had been joined by the nonparticipant within the empire itself. The aristocrat would pass from reassuringly similar forum to forum, speaking a uniform language, observing rites and codes of behavior shared by all educated men; but his road stretched through the territories of tribesmen that were as alien to him as any German or Persian. In Gaul, the country-men still spoke Celtic; in North Africa, Punic and Libyan; in Asia Minor, ancient dialects such as Lycaonian, Phrygian and Cappadocian; in Syria, Aramaic and Syriac.

Living cheek by jowl with this immense unabsorbed "barbarian" world, the governing classes of the Roman Empire had kept largely free of some of the more virulent exclusiveness of modern colonial regimes: they were notoriously tolerant of race and of local religions. But the price they demanded for inclusion in their own world was conformity—the adoption of its style of life, of its traditions, of its education, and so of its two classical languages, Latin in the West and Greek in the East. Those who were in no position to participate were dismissed: they were frankly despised as "country-bumpkins" and "barbarians." Those who could have participated and did not—most notably the Jews—were treated with varying degrees of hatred and contempt, only occasionally tempered by respectful curiosity for the representatives of an ancient Near Eastern civilization. Those who had once participated and had ostentatiously "dropped out"—namely the Christians—were liable to summary execution. By A.D. 200 many provincial governors and many mobs had had occasion to assert the boundaries of the classical world with hysterical certainty against the Christian dissenter in their midst: as one magistrate told Christians, "I cannot bring myself so much as to listen to people who speak ill of the Roman way of religion."

Classical society of about A.D. 200 was a society with firm boundaries. Yet it was far from being a stagnant society. In the Greek world, the classical tradition had already existed for some seven hundred years. Its first burst of creativity, at Athens, should not blind us to the astonishing way in which, from the time of the conquests of Alexander the Great, Greek culture had settled down to a rhythm of survival—as drawn-out, as capable of exquisite nuance as patient of repetition as a plain-chant. One exciting renaissance had taken place in the second century A.D. It coincided with a revival of the economic life and the political initiative of the upper classes of the Greek cities. The age of the Antonines was the heyday of the Greek Sophists. These men—known for their devotion to rhetoric—were at one and the same time literary lions and great urban nabobs. They enjoyed vast influence and popularity: one of them, Polemo of Smyrna, "treated whole cities as his inferiors, emperors as not his superiors and gods . . . as equals." Behind them stood the thriving cities of the Aegean. The huge classical remains at Ephesus and Smyrna (and, indeed, similar contemporary cities and temples, from Lepcis Magna in Tunisia to Baalbek in the Lebanon) seem to us nowadays to sum up a timeless ancient world. They were, in fact, the creation of only a few generations of baroque magnificence, between Hadrian (117–138) and Septimius Severus (193–211).

It is just at the end of the second and the beginning of the third centuries, also, that the Greek culture was garnered which formed the ballast of the classical tradition throughout the Middle Ages. The encyclopedias, the handbooks of medicine, natural science and astronomy, to which all cultivated men—Latins, Byzantines, Arabs—turned for the next fifteen hundred years, were compiled then. Literary tastes and political attitudes that continued, in the Greek world, until the end of the Middle Ages, were first formed in the age of the Antonines: Byzantine gentlemen of the fifteenth century were still using a recondite Attic Greek deployed by the Sophists of the age of Hadrian.

At this time the Greek world made the Roman Empire its own. We can appreciate this identification with the Roman state and the subtle shifts of emphasis it entailed, by looking at a Greek from Bithynia, who had joined the Roman governing class as a senator—Dio Cassius, who wrote his *Roman History* up to A.D. 229. No matter how enthusiastically Dio had absorbed the outlook of the Roman Senate, we are constantly reminded that the empire had come to Greeks accustomed to centuries of enlightened despotism. Dio knew that the Roman emperor was an autocrat. Common decency and a shared interest with the educated upper classes were the only checks on his behavior—not the delicate clockwork of the constitution of Augustus. And Dio knew how fragile such restraints could be: he had been present at a meeting of the Senate when an astrologer had denounced certain "bald-pated men" for conspiring against the emperor . . . instinctively his hand had shot up to feel the top of his head. But Dio accepted the strong rule of one man as long as it gave him an orderly world: only the emperor could suppress civil war; only he could police the faction-ridden Greek cities; only he could make Dio's class secure and respected. Byzantine scholars who turned to Dio, centuries later, to know about Roman history, found themselves hopelessly at sea in his account of the heroes of the Roman republic:

but they were able to understand perfectly the strong and conscientious emperors of Dio's own age—already the Roman history of a Greek of the late second and early third century A.D. was *their* history.

A shift of the center of gravity of the Roman Empire towards the Greek cities of Asia Minor, a flowering of a Greek mandarinate—in these ways, the palmy days of the Antonines already point in the direction of Byzantium. But the men of the age of Dio Cassius still resolutely faced the other way: they were stalwart conservatives; their greatest successes had been expressed in a cultural reaction; for them, the boundaries of the classical world were still clear and rigid—Byzantium proper, a civilization that could build, on top of this ancient backward-looking tradition, such revolutionary novelties as the establishment of Christianity and the foundation of Constantinople as a "New Rome," was inconceivable to a man like Dio. (He never, for instance, so much as mentions the existence of Christianity, although Christians had worried the authorities in his home-country for over 150 years.) Such a civilization could only emerge in the late Roman revolution of the third and fourth centuries A.D.

*   *   *

The theme that will emerge throughout this book is the shifting and redefinition of the boundaries of the classical world after A.D. 200. This has little to do with the conventional problem of the "Decline and Fall of the Roman Empire." The "Decline and Fall" affected only the political structure of the western provinces of the Roman Empire: it left the cultural powerhouse of Late Antiquity—the eastern Mediterranean and the Near East—unscathed. Even in the barbarian states of western Europe, in the sixth and seventh centuries, the Roman Empire, as it survived at Constantinople, was still regarded as the greatest civilized state in the world: and it was called by its ancient name, the *Respublica*. The problem that urgently preoccupied men of Late Antiquity themselves was, rather, the painful modification of the ancient boundaries.

Geographically, the hold of the Mediterranean slackened. After 410 Britain was abandoned; after 480 Gaul came to be firmly ruled from the north. In the East, paradoxically, the rolling back of the Mediterranean had happened earlier and more imperceptibly; but it proved decisive. Up to the first century A.D., a veneer of Greek civilization still covered large areas of the Iranian plateau: a Greco-Buddhist art had flourished in Afghanistan, and the decrees of a Buddhist ruler have been found outside Kabul, translated into impeccable philosophical Greek. In 224, however, a family from Fars, the "Deep South" of Iranian chauvinism, gained control of the Persian Empire. The revived Persian Empire of this, the Sassanian, dynasty quickly shook the Greek fancy-dress from its shoulders. An efficient and aggressive empire, whose ruling classes were notably unreceptive to western influence, now stood on the eastern frontiers of the Roman Empire. In 252, 257 and again in 260, the great Shahanshah, the king of kings, Shapur I, showed what terrible damage his mailed horsemen could do:

> *Valerian the Caesar came against us with seventy thousand men . . . and we fought a great battle against him, and we took Valerian the Caesar with our own hands. . . . And the provinces of Syria, Cilicia and Cappadocia we burnt with fire, we ravaged and conquered them, taking their peoples captive.*

The fear of repeating such an experience tilted the balance of the emperor's concern further from the Rhine and ever nearer to the Euphrates. What is more, the confrontation with Sassanian Persia breached the barriers of the classical world in the Near East: for it gave prominence to Mesopotamia, and so exposed the Roman world to constant influence from that area of immense, exotic creativity in art and religion.

It is not always the conventional dates that are the most decisive. Everyone knows that the Goths sacked Rome in 410: but the lost western provinces of the empire remained a recognizably "sub-Roman" civilization for centuries. By contrast, when the eastern provinces of the empire were lost to Islam after 640, these did not long remain "sub-Byzantine" societies: they were rapidly "orientalized." For Islam itself was pulled far to the east of its original conquests by the vast mass of the conquered Persian Empire. In the eighth century the Mediterranean seaboard came to be ruled from Baghdad; the Mediterranean became a backwater to men who were used to sailing from the Persian Gulf; and the court of Harun al-Rashid (788–809), with its heavy trappings of "sub-Persian" culture, was a reminder that the irreversible victory of the Near East over the Greeks began slowly but surely with the revolt of Fars in A.D. 224.

As the Mediterranean receded, so a more ancient world came to light. Craftsmen in Britain returned to the art forms of the La Tène age. The serf of late Roman Gaul reemerged with his Celtic name— the *vassus*. The arbiters of piety of the Roman world, the Coptic hermits of Egypt, revived the language of the Pharaohs; and the hymn-writers of Syria heaped on Christ appellations of Divine King-ship that reach back to Sumerian times. Round the Mediterranean itself, inner barriers collapsed. Another side of the Roman world, often long prepared in obscurity, came to the top, like different-colored loam turned by the plow. Three generations after Dio Cassius had ignored it, Christianity became the religion of the emperors. Small things sometimes betray changes more faithfully, because un-consciously. Near Rome, a sculptor's yard of the fourth century still turned out statues, impeccably dressed in the old Roman toga (with a socket for detachable portrait-heads!); but the aristocrats who com-missioned such works would, in fact, wear a costume which betrayed prolonged exposure to the "barbarians" of the non-Mediterranean world—a woollen shirt from the Danube, a cloak from northern Gaul, fastened at the shoulders by a filigree brooch from Germany, even guarding their health by "Saxon" trousers. Deeper still, at the very core of the Mediterranean, the tradition of Greek philosophy had found a way of opening itself to a different religious mood.

Such changes as these are the main themes of the evolution of the Late Antique world.

Ramsay MacMullen
SOCIAL TRANSFORMATION

The purpose of this book is to show how energies both harmonious and hostile to the Roman order appeared in a given class at a given time. As the locus of these energies moved down the social scale in the course of the first four centuries of the Empire, so the enemies of the state were, to begin with, drawn from senatorial ranks and, in the end, from peasants and barbarians. The drift of directing power outward and downward from the Roman aristocracy is well known; its corollary is the simultaneous movement of anti-Establishment impulses in the same direction. I can see no significant struggle of slave against free or poor against rich. Protest originated within whatever classes were dominant at different periods. Perhaps that is what we should expect. The French Revolution, favorite cadaver for historical dissection, offers all the signs of a narrowly internal disease, the bourgeois fomenting reforms of a system they themselves controlled. The phenomenon is typical. History, as it is not one of the semiexact, or social, sciences, does not easily accommodate theories; people, *deo gratias,* retain the right to be puzzling; but the patterns detected here seem to fit times and peoples other than Roman.

At any rate, when the story of the empire begins, it is men like Brutus who crowd the councils of the monarch, and who murder monarchy, as they think, on the Ides of March. Had Caesar been able to tell friends from foes, he would have survived that day, but they appeared identical down to the smallest detail of family and origin, of earlier careers and training, of accent and dress, of enthusiasm for a good prose style that Caesar ardently shared. A century later the descendants of this group of pro- and anti-Caesarians, somewhat mixed now with a newer nobility, were still supplying both supporters and destroyers of the throne, the two so similar that in fact many members of one allegiance—Seneca or Lucan, let us say—passed over to the other without giving up any essential belief. There have always been men who switched sides, of course; they have often

166

insisted that it was rather the rest of the world that changed, not themselves; still, it is striking how interchangeable and ambiguous were the attitudes of the different groups in the aristocracy, how Janus-faced they were, looking toward the past, *libertas,* and senate, and at the same time toward the future, stability, and the emperor. The emperor himself often cultivated the literature that nerved his subjects to speak out, the astrology that they pursued at the risk of capital punishment, and the rhetorical exercises that extolled tyrannicide. Literature, astrology, and rhetoric, like their practitioners, were sources of possible danger to the throne. They were also characteristic to the Roman establishment. Add the old families, political marriages, and Stoicism. The operation of these latter factors, too, in the circles of the emperor's enemies, is obvious.

In sources for the history of the opposition in the first century, that is, in Tacitus above all, and Seneca, and Pliny, the dominant figures are men of high birth whose home is Italy. The making of events belongs to them even if their dearest ambition sometimes seems to be the unmaking of events and the return to an age long past, whether Cato's or Zeno's or Aristogeiton's. Succeeding generations admitted an increasing admixture of recruits to the inner circle of influence. Tacitus's family may have come from southern Gaul, Seneca's was Spanish. In the second century the very emperors were no longer exclusively Italian. Their friends—Herodes Atticus, Avidius Cassius—might be Greek or Syrian. Opening opportunities for colonials by no means guaranteed their loyalty. Herodes participated in a movement, the so-called Second Sophistic, perfectly harmless on the surface but anti-Roman in its implications, since its intent was the reassertion of Hellenism. As for Avidius Cassius, he rebelled, getting help from his countrymen. For a time thereafter an attempt was made to assign officers to provinces other than those of their birth. Events proved the precaution pointless and it was abandoned. The list of revolts and pretenders over the next two hundred years reveals no pattern of "Syria for the Syrians" or of aid given only to native sons. Not separatism but power without definition found expression as much in Herodes Atticus as in Cassius; for the first benefit of power has always been to use it as one pleases. Once a share had passed from the more generous or slackening grasp of Tacitus's like to a wider circle, it was destined to appear embodied in a thousand shapes, some harmonious with the historic aims and character of

Rome, some otherwise. The provincial elite under the Antonines played on a far wider stage the same ambiguous role as the older Roman elite had played in the capital a century earlier.

Developments that gave a chance to leaders in the provinces to assert themselves worked equally in favor of once-despised classes in Italy as everywhere else. They attained wealth and influence without wholly abandoning their inheritance. A love of gaudily colored clothes, for example, slowly grew upon the upper classes, though much of the style seems to have originated among circus habitués. In the Greek East, plebeian enthusiasms for gladiation in the end infected the aristocracy. As medical science stagnated, a scum of superstition rose to the surface: the gods could reveal cures in dreams, hence the crowds of consulars thronging the shrines of Asclepius as never before, to talk to him, and no doubt ceaselessly to each other, about their stomach disorders and arthritic joints. The number and artistry of amulets rises in the third and fourth centuries. St. Basil assumes their popularity in his congregation. "Is your boy sick? Then you search out the incantation expert, or someone who will put a charm with curious characters on it around the necks of innocent children"—such a charm, perhaps, as the encyclopedic authority of Alexander of Tralles recommended for colic, to be worn as a necklace or a ring; while at the other extremity of the empire, a Gallic peasant who got something stuck in his throat invoked his ancestral gods in Celtic in a spell duly recorded by medical handbooks: "Rub out of the throat, out of the gullet, Aisus, remove thou thyself my evil out of the throat, out of the gorge."

Testimony here to the rise of popular culture into the ruling classes; testimony also to the tenacious conservatism characterizing beliefs in the supernatural. As Celtic, a language living only among the poor and the isolated, found its way into books in the form of an incantation, so the last inscriptions in Phrygian, of the third century, are predominantly curse formulas; and of a similar nature, by the third century, the development of a usable alphabet for the Egyptian tongue answered the needs of religion and its literature embodied in various hagiologies and Last Judgment scenes a great deal of the fellahin's immemorial dreads, visions, and symbols. Archeologists working with a totally different kind of evidence report parallel findings. The dominant culture of the empire exerted its strongest influence on the material plane, while unmaterial aspects such as cults and superstitions remained least affected. If Romanization worked least on the unmaterial plane, it follows that an un-Roman religion, Christianity, attaining riches and power, could elevate with it to official favor the beliefs and tastes that had laid hitherto hidden away among the masses. That conclusion can in fact be confirmed through the study of such scattered subjects as late antique art, literary metaphors, and ideas of social justice.

The life that Tacitus knew because he saw it among the tenant farmers who worked his fields, or among the troops that he must surely have commanded at some time in his career, had its own force of growth needing only the stimulation of opportunity to express itself through its risen heroes: peasants chosen as abbots, freedman become municipal councilors, the sons of barbarian irregulars clothed with high government office by that loosening of society typical of the third century and still effective in the fourth. Tacitus, however, would have insisted that Roman civilization meant something higher and narrower: the capital; more, the great within it; eloquence and philology; the Ara Pacis and the Temple of Concord. It was from this world that rules reached down to give structure to the life of the masses.

With consensus very flattering to Tacitus's smugness, modern assessments of what Rome achieved emphasize much the same things; but the distortion here is evident. What is outstanding is by definition untypical; what rules forbid does not cease to exist. No doubt illegal resorts to magic were more important to the bulk of the population than visits to publicly acknowledged divinities, even though less obvious in our sources. Relative lack of evidence proves nothing. Consider, by way of analogy, how much of today's literature and how rich a selection of material remains might be known without ever hinting at the modern popularity of gambling. Equally true of many private associations, lacking even a name, simply friends and neighbors meeting every Monday afternoon, now as then hardly the concern of historians. Inhabitants of the Roman Empire were continually forming clubs of every conceivable description, despite laws that might, for all their elasticity, be at any moment invoked against them. And again, despite legislation that forbade slander or treasonous publications, the ordinary citizen told his rulers what he thought of them in furtive doggerel posted on statues or, safe in a crowd, in rhythmic shouts at the theater. This was democracy, of a sort; clubs demonstrated sociability; and superstition demonstrated religiosity—all three, aspects of popular culture, and not a whit less Roman for being actually illegal. In the later Empire, all three were admitted to a public role. Membership in associations was positively enforced; whole cities bought amulets to ward off plagues and earthquakes; and leaders of Church and state had their cause noised abroad in polemical songs or in the unison chanting of some theatrical or senatorial audience: " 'Claudius Augustus, may the gods preserve you,' said sixty times; 'Claudius Augustus, you or your like we have always desired as emperor,' said forty times.''

Rostovtzeff ended his incomparable *Social and Economic History of the Roman Empire* with two famous questions: "Is it possible to extend a higher civilization to the lower classes without debasing its standard and diluting its quality to the vanishing point? Is not every civilization bound to decay as soon as it begins to penetrate the masses?'' The assumption behind his despair is Tacitean: there is one drop of purple—let us take that, the color of the senatorial stripe and, for Epictetus, the blazon of moral eminence—one drop of purple in a pool of water. Dilution destroys it. But, as Rostovtzeff showed better than anyone else has done, civilization is the whole pool, and all its levels possess a distinctive color. Pursuits of the lower classes forbidden by the nobility or excluded by them from what they would have defined as Roman nevertheless had their own vital principle. The unlawful and un-Roman can be kept out of history only if it is written by people of the purple stripe.

Illyricum supplies a final illustration of what I am getting at. Here (less clearly than in the Rhine provinces, to be sure) archeologists have discovered traces of decorative arts driven off the field by the competition of classicizing tastes in the first and earlier second centuries, reclaiming a part of their popularity in the late second, third, and fourth centuries, and joining other local customs and beliefs which had never been much changed to form a cultural whole. This latter was certainly un-Roman, though not in any aggressive sense of the term. Yet the same area and the same population produced the savior dynasties of the later Empire. They appeared before the middle of the third century, tightened their grip on power right through the fourth century, and over that long, long duration of crisis succeeded in keeping far more hostile and un-Roman forces than themselves at bay. Was Illyricum un-Roman, then? No more than the senate of the first century, from which came the enemies of the state as well as its chief upholders. What had occurred in the interval was a shift in the locus of energy. Its causes do not concern us here. Its effects are detectable in the increasing prominence of actors barely participant in the drama of the earlier Empire, gradually coming forward to the center of the stage. Sometimes they appeared as aberrant or destructive to the civilization in which they originated; they have then supplied the chief focus for this book; at other times they spoke, as it were, for the majority; but in either case, the broad lines of Roman and un-Roman history trace the same course.

IV LESSONS FOR THE FUTURE

Edward Gibbon
SAFETY FROM BARBARIAN ATTACK

This awful revolution may be usefully applied to the instruction of the present age. It is the duty of a patriot to prefer and promote the exclusive interest and glory of his native country; but a philosopher may be permitted to enlarge his views, and to consider Europe as one great republic, whose various inhabitants have attained almost the same level of politeness and cultivation. The balance of power will continue to fluctuate, and the prosperity of our own or the neighboring kingdoms may be alternately exalted or depressed; but these partial events cannot essentially injure our general state of happiness, the system of arts, and laws, and manners, which so advantageously distinguish, above the rest of mankind, the Europeans and their colonies. The savage nations of the globe are the common enemies of civilized society; and we may inquire with anxious curiosity, whether Europe is still threatened with a repetition of those calamities which formerly oppressed the arms and institutions of Rome. Perhaps the same reflections will illustrate the fall of that mighty empire, and explain the probable causes of our actual security.

I. The Romans were ignorant of the extent of their danger, and the number of their enemies. Beyond the Rhine and Danube, the northern countries of Europe and Asia were filled with innumerable tribes of hunters and shepherds, poor, voracious, and turbulent; bold in arms, and impatient to ravish the fruits of industry. The Barbarian world was agitated by the rapid impulse of war; and the peace of Gaul or Italy was shaken by the distant revolutions of China. The Huns, who fled before a victorious enemy, directed their march towards the West; and the torrent was swelled by the gradual accession of captives and allies. The flying tribes who yielded to the Huns assumed in *their* turn the spirit of conquest; the endless column of Barbarians pressed on the Roman Empire with accumulated weight; and, if the foremost were destroyed, the vacant space was instantly replenished by new assailants. Such formidable emigrations can no longer issue from the North; and the long repose, which has been

From Edward Gibbon, *Decline and Fall of the Roman Empire* (London, 1901), Vol. IV, pp. 163–69. For the context of this selection, see above, pp. 19–22.

imputed to the decrease of population, is the happy consequence of the progress of arts and agriculture. Instead of some rude villages, thinly scattered among its woods and morasses, Germany now produces a list of two thousand three hundred walled towns; the Christian kingdoms of Denmark, Sweden, and Poland, have been successively established; and the Hanse merchants, with the Teutonic knights, have extended their colonies along the coast of the Baltic, as far as the Gulf of Finland. From the Gulf of Finland to the Eastern Ocean, Russia now assumes the form of a powerful and civilized empire. The plow, the loom, and the forge, are introduced on the banks of the Volga, the Oby, and the Lena; and the fiercest of the Tartar hordes have been taught to tremble and obey. The reign of independent Barbarism is now contracted to a narrow span; and the remnant of Calmucks or Uzbecks, whose forces may be almost numbered, cannot seriously excite the apprehensions of the great republic of Europe. Yet this apparent security should not tempt us to forget that new enemies, and unknown dangers, may *possibly* arise from some obscure people, scarcely visible in the map of the world. The Arabs or Saracens, who spread their conquests from India to Spain, had languished in poverty and contempt, till Mahomet breathed into those savage bodies the soul of enthusiasm.

II. The empire of Rome was firmly established by the singular and perfect coalition of its members. The subject nations, resigning the hope, and even the wish, of independence, embraced the character of Roman citizens; and the provinces of the West were reluctantly torn by the Barbarians from the bosom of their mother-country. But this union was purchased by the loss of national freedom and military spirit; and the servile provinces, destitute of life and motion, expected their safety from the mercenary troops and governors, who were directed by the orders of a distant court. The happiness of an hundred millions depended on the personal merit of one or two men, perhaps children, whose minds were corrupted by education, luxury, and despotic power. The deepest wounds were inflicted on the empire during the minorities of the sons and grandsons of Theodosius; and, after those incapable princes seemed to attain the age of manhood, they abandoned the church to the bishops, the state to the eunuchs, and the provinces to the Barbarians. Europe is now divided into twelve powerful, though unequal, kingdoms, three respectable commonwealths, and a variety of smaller, though independent, states; the chances of royal and ministerial talents are multiplied, at least with the number of its rulers; and a Julian, or Semiramis, may reign in the North, while Arcadius and Honorius again slumber on the thrones of the South. The abuses of tyranny are restrained by the mutual influence of fear and shame; republics have acquired order and stability; monarchies have imbibed the principles of freedom, or, at least, of moderation; and some sense of honor and justice is introduced into the most defective constitutions by the general manners of the times. In peace, the progress of knowledge and industry is accelerated by the emulation of so many active rivals: in war, the European forces are exercised by temperate and undecisive contests. If a savage conqueror should issue from the deserts of Tartary, he must repeatedly vanquish the robust peasants of Russia, the numerous armies of Germany, the gallant nobles of France, and the intrepid freemen of Britain; who, perhaps, might confederate for their common defense. Should the victorious Barbarians carry slavery and desolation as far as the Atlantic Ocean, ten thousand vessels would transport beyond their pursuit the remains of civilized society; and Europe would revive and flourish in the American world, which is already filled with her colonies and institutions.

III. Cold, poverty, and a life of danger and fatigue, fortify the strength and courage of Barbarians. In every age they have oppressed the polite and peaceful nations of China, India, and Persia, who neglected, and still neglect, to counterbalance these natural powers by the resources of military art. The warlike states of antiquity, Greece, Macedonia, and Rome, educated a race of soldiers; exercised their bodies, disciplined their courage, multiplied their forces by regular evolutions, and converted the iron which they possessed, into strong and serviceable weapons. But this superiority insensibly declined with their laws and manners; and the feeble policy of Constantine and his successors armed and instructed, for the ruin of the empire, the rude valor of the Barbarian mercenaries. The military art has been changed by the invention of gunpowder; which enables man to command the two most powerful agents of nature, air and fire. Mathematics, chemistry, mechanics, architecture, have been applied to the service of war; and the adverse parties oppose to each other the most elaborate modes of attack and of defense. Historians may indignantly observe that the preparations of a siege would found and maintain a flourishing colony; yet we cannot be displeased that the subversion of a city should be a work of cost and difficulty, or that an industrious people should be protected by those arts, which survive and supply the decay of military virtue. Cannon and fortifications now form an impregnable barrier against the Tartar horse; and Europe is secure from any future irruption of Barbarians; since, before they can conquer, they must cease to be barbarous. Their gradual advances in the science of war would always be accompanied, as we may learn from the example of Russia, with a proportionable improvement in the arts of peace and civil policy; and they themselves must deserve a place among the polished nations whom they subdue.

Should these speculations be found doubtful or fallacious, there still remains a more humble source of comfort and hope. The discoveries of ancient and modern navigators, and the domestic history, or tradition, of the most enlightened nations, represent the *human savage,* naked both in mind and body, and destitute of laws, of arts, of ideas, and almost of language. From this abject condition, perhaps the primitive and universal state of man, he has gradually arisen to command the animals, to fertilize the earth, to traverse the ocean, and to measure the heavens. His progress in the improvement and exercise of his mental and corporeal faculties has been irregular and various, infinitely slow in the beginning, and increasing by degrees with redoubled velocity; ages of laborious ascent have been followed by a moment of rapid downfall; and the several climates of the globe have felt the vicissitudes of light and darkness. Yet the experience of four thousand years should enlarge our hopes, and diminish our apprehensions; we cannot determine to what height the human species may aspire in their advances towards perfection; but it may safely be presumed that no people, unless the face of nature is changed, will relapse into their original barbarism. The improvements of society may be viewed under a threefold aspect. (1) The poet or philosopher illustrates his age and country by the efforts of a *single* mind; but these superior powers of reason or fancy are rare and spontaneous productions, and the genius of Homer, or Cicero, or Newton, would excite less admiration, if they could be created by the will of a prince or the lessons of a preceptor. (2) The benefits of law and policy, of trade and manufactures, of arts and sciences, are more solid and permanent; and *many* individuals may be qualified, by education and discipline, to promote, in their respective stations, the interest of the community. But this general order is the effect of skill and labor; and the complex machinery may be decayed by time or injured by violence. (3) Fortunately for mankind, the more useful, or, at least, more necessary arts can be performed without superior talents or national subordination; without the powers of *one* or the union of *many*. Each village, each family, each individual, must always possess both ability and inclination to perpetuate the use of fire and of metals; the propagation and service of domestic animals; the methods of hunting and fishing; the rudiments of navigation; the imperfect cultivation of corn or other nutritive grain; and the simple practice of the mechanic trades. Private genius and public industry may be extirpated; but these hardy plants survive the tempest, and strike an everlasting root into the most unfavorable soil. The splendid days of Augustus and Trajan were eclipsed by a cloud of ignorance; and the Barbarians subverted the laws and palaces of Rome. But the scythe, the invention or emblem of Saturn, still continued annually to mow the harvests of Italy; and the human feasts of the Læstrygons have never been renewed on the coast of Campania.

Since the first discovery of the arts, war, commerce, and religious zeal have diffused, among the savages of the Old and New World, those inestimable gifts: they have been successively propagated; they can never be lost. We may therefore acquiesce in the pleasing conclusion that every age of the world has increased, and still increases, the real wealth, the happiness, the knowledge, and perhaps the virtue, of the human race.

W. E. Heitland
POPULAR GOVERNMENT

The only means known to us of combating evil and promoting good in a community with any prospect of lasting success lies in the action of the popular will clearly, freely and continuously expressed. This is

From W. E. Heitland, *The Roman Fate* (Cambridge, England, 1922), p. 80, by permission of the Cambridge University Press.

Politics, to bear a part in which is a citizen's duty. Rome is merely an extreme instance of failure from lack of this means of regeneration. Perhaps the failure would have occurred, even had the means been available: but it was not there, and so could not be tried.

This principle is true for all states in all ages, and History, recording endless failures, is one long record of this truth. To improve your citizens, and to interest them in their own real welfare, is the only course that offers a possible means of avoiding the Roman fate.

Michael I. Rostovtzeff

INCLUSION OF THE MASSES

None of the existing theories fully explains the problem of the decay of ancient civilization, if we can apply the word "decay" to the complex phenomenon which I have endeavored to describe. Each of them, however, has contributed much to the clearing of the ground, and has helped us to perceive that the main phenomenon which underlies the process of decline is the gradual absorption of the educated classes by the masses and the consequent simplification of all the functions of political, social, economic, and intellectual life, which we call the barbarization of the ancient world.

The evolution of the ancient world has a lesson and a warning for us. Our civilization will not last unless it be a civilization not of one class, but of the masses. The Oriental civilizations were more stable and lasting than the Greco-Roman, because, being chiefly based on religion, they were nearer to the masses. Another lesson is that violent attempts at leveling have never helped to uplift the masses. They have destroyed the upper classes, and resulted in accelerating the process of barbarization. But the ultimate problem remains like a ghost, ever present and unlaid: Is it possible to extend a higher civilization to the lower classes without debasing its standard and diluting its quality to the vanishing point? Is not every civilization bound to decay as soon as it begins to penetrate the masses?

F. W. Walbank
A PLANNED AND JUST SOCIETY

In one way or another our own society has incorporated within its texture all that matters of classical culture and the culture of still earlier civilizations. The decline and fall of Rome was real enough, a genuine decay springing from a complex of causes that are only too painfully clear. Yet, for all that, it was the route along which humanity passed, through the long apparent stagnation of feudalism to that fresh burst of progress, which created the modern world. And now, having advanced, not indeed along that straight upward line of which we spoke in an earlier chapter, but by the time-honored method of one step backwards, two steps forwards, we find ourselves once more standing at the crossroads and turning with Gibbon to read anew the lesson of the decline of Rome.

"This awful revolution," he wrote, "may be usefully applied to the instruction of the present age." What then are the alternatives which it indicates for us? They are not in doubt. One choice that confronts us is to plan the resources of our society for the whole of our peoples, whether black or white; to rid ourselves of the menace of underconsumption, that incubus which we share with the Roman Empire; to effect a more equitable distribution of wealth; and to give full scope for the employment of the new technical forces man already controls. This is a new path along which antiquity cannot light us, because it never trod that way. The alternative is to ignore the lesson which history offers, to follow in the footsteps of the ancient world (which never solved this problem because it could not), to plan—or fail to plan—for the few, for underconsumption at home, for a scramble after markets abroad, and so eventually for further, deadlier wars and ultimate ruin.

That this ruin might, like the ruin of Rome, give rise to new social developments, leading in the fulness of time to some future society, which would in turn be presented with the same problem, is little consolation to us if we fail now. But because we have the choice, where the ancients had none, let us be more charitable as we contemplate their downfall and the inexorable chain of cause and effect,

From F. W. Walbank, *The Decline of the Roman Empire in the West* (New York, 1953), pp. 84–85, by permission of Lawrence & Wishart Ltd.

as it operated throughout the whole of the social structure of antiquity. Let us avoid taking sides hastily, either with the Emperors, who were salvaging at a heavy price the remnants of civilization in the only way open to them, or with their utopian enemies who, from altruistic or selfish motives, fought to extort an individual freedom which society could not grant. Instead of solacing ourselves with the passing of moral judgments on those who are now long since dead, we shall do better to be quite sure that we know why ancient society declined to an inevitable end; and, having learned the lesson of that "awful revolution," we may reserve our passions and our energies for the more immediate task of helping to right what is wrong in our own civilization.

Michael Grant
INTERNAL HARMONY

The first section of this volume [*Fall of the Roman Empire: A Reappraisal*] briefly surveyed the course of events up to the downfall of Rome in the West, particularly concentrating upon its last hundred and twelve years, in which the Empire crumbled from its former mighty power and size and was eventually destroyed at the hands of its eternal enemies.

But this failure in face of the foe need never have occurred had it not been for internal disunities within the Empire itself. And so an endeavor has here been made to identify and describe these rifts, and to show how they fatally undermined resistance to the invaders, so that rapid collapse ensued. Every one of the same afflictions, in a more or less advanced stage, can be detected in our own modern societies as well, so that it is a matter of imperative topical interest to note the guidances and the warnings which the ancient developments are able to afford us.

It has proved possible to identify thirteen of the fissures which rent the ancient Roman Empire, and which may likewise shatter our modern world as well. The first, the confrontation and suppression of governments by military men, is an ill which the United States and Britain do not suffer from, but which endangers the stability of the entire world because of its prevalence elsewhere. For the other disunities, however, which disrupted the Roman Empire, we have to look no further than our own fragmented American and British communities to find the very same phenomena in more or less developed forms. Misery among the poor continues to exist. The large sums expended on the armed forces do not always have popular support. The rich include many who pursue their own interests at the national expense. The middle class, as our current economic crises develop, are among the worst sufferers. And, in the same process, there is a danger that, as in the ancient world, the inevitably expanding bureaucracy will get out of control and become alienated from the rest of the population, with counterproductive results. Moreover, like the Emperors of Rome, our Presidents and Prime Ministers can all too readily become isolated from the thoughts, feelings and loyalties of their subjects.

All these acute disharmonies that exist, or threaten to exist, in our own time were already powerful factors contributing to the disruption of the Roman world. . . .

Then we came to the gulf which separated and estranged those natural allies, the two Roman Empires, from one another, with fatally weakening effects which inspire the hope that Western Europe and America will not similarly reject their necessary task of collaboration today.

A further disastrous failure, the failure to seize the chance of cooperative partnership between the Romans and the numerous immigrants in their midst, highlights, once again, a current problem common to the United States and European countries, which so urgently need to assimilate or satisfy their own alienated ethnic minorities.

[There were] more insidious blows to the unity of the Roman Empire. The first was delivered by the dropouts, men and women who, like their counterparts today, abandoned society altogether, and went to live right outside it, thus depriving the state of manpower and revenue. The second blow was struck by the government itself, which tried to coerce dissidents by force, thus making the existing divisions far more serious than they had been before. Finally, . . . two wide-spread attitudes of mind . . . likewise made their contribution to national collapse. First, there was the complacent traditionalism which, looking at the past, concluded that everything would come right in the end and that no novel methods were needed to ensure that this happy result should materialize. And secondly, there was the suggestion that, owing to the overriding importance of quite other, spiritual considerations, no particular efforts need or should be devoted to the pressing problems that were undermining the terrestrial world of Rome. Both of these phenomena are found today: a foolish form of patriotism which relies unconstructively on the past, and a deficiency of that minimum of patriotism required to enable the world, as we know it, to survive.

Such are the flaws in our own structure, flaws which this book has sought to identify in ancient Rome as well. Looking back at the Romans, we can try to close the gaps that separate one group and interest from another in our own society. Yet although its resemblances to the society of declining Rome are so numerous and powerful, that does not mean it is inevitable for us to succumb to the same fate as the Romans did. It is not necessarily, in the words of Cyril Connolly, closing time in the gardens of the West. There is nothing inevitable about the process at all. As Maxim Gorki insisted, man has to understand that he is the creator, controller and master of civilization, and that the decision whether things turn out badly or not so badly rests with himself. The history of the Romans is what they made of it; what we make of our own history is likewise our own choice.

What has to be done, therefore, is to make sure that the disunities which pulled the Romans apart, and which are disquietingly identifiable, one after another, in our own world, do not shatter our civilization as well. The remark of Benjamin Franklin . . . remains as appropriate as ever: "Yes, we must indeed all hang together, or, most assuredly, we shall all hang separately."

Suggestions for Additional Reading

The best introduction to the problem remains Edward Gibbon's *Decline and Fall of the Roman Empire*, in the J. B. Bury edition (7 vols., London, 1909–1914). For an up-to-date and thorough study of the late empire the student can now consult A. H. M. Jones, *The Later Roman Empire, 248–602 A.D.* (3 vols., Oxford, 1964). *The Decline of the Ancient World* (London, 1966) is a shortened and simplified version of this work. Another work of fundamental importance is Fergus Millar's *The Roman Empire and Its Neighbors* (London, 1967). There are several good one-volume studies of Roman history: A. E. R. Boak and W. G. Sinnigen, *History of Rome to 565 A.D.* (5th ed., New York, 1965); M. Cary and H. H. Scullard, *A History of Rome* (3rd ed., New York, 1976); F. M. Heichelheim and C. A. Yeo, *A History of the Roman People* (Englewood Cliffs, New Jersey, 1962). For the early imperial period a detailed narrative account is provided by J. B. Bury's *A History of the Roman Empire from Its Foundation to the Death of Marcus Aurelius* (27 B.C.–180 A.D.), London, 1900). A brief but excellent account of the first three centuries of the empire is to be found in M. P. Charlesworth's *The Roman Empire* (London, 1951). The fourth century is usually treated in connection with the problem of transition to the Middle Ages, but there are several special studies of it. Piganiol's *L'Empire Chretien* (Paris, 1947) gives a detailed and thorough account. Another useful one-volume treatment of the late empire is H. M. D. Parker's *A History of the Roman World from A.D. 138 to 337*, rev. by B. H. Warmington (London, 1969).

Our understanding of Roman social history has come a long way since the pioneering work of Samuel Dill, *Roman Society in the Last Century of the Western Empire* (2nd ed., London, 1899). Some of the most interesting work is that of Ramsay MacMullen in a series of monographs: *Soldier and Civilian in the Later Roman Empire* (Cambridge, Mass., 1967); *Enemies of the Roman Order* (Cambridge, Mass., 1966); *Roman Social Relations 50 B.C. to A.D. 284* (New Haven, 1974); *Roman Governments' Response to Crisis, A.D. 285–337* (New Haven, 1976). For an understanding of intellectual life in the empire, T. R. Glover's *Life and Literature in the Fourth Century* (Cambridge, 1901) and C. G. Starr's *Civilization and the Caesars: The Intellectual Revolution in the Roman Empire* (Ithaca, 1954) are useful. Sir Ronald Syme's *Ammianus and the Historia Augusta* (Oxford, 1968) and Alan

Cameron's *Claudian* (Oxford, 1970) are recent studies of important figures in the intellectual life of the late empire.

The problem of transition from the ancient to the medieval world has received much attention. The first two volumes of the *Cambridge Medieval History* (2nd ed., Cambridge, 1936) contain detailed studies by specialists. A good narrative is provided by J. B. Bury, *History of the Later Roman Empire, 395–565* (2 vols., London, 1923). The idea that there was any "decline" or "fall" or "ruin" has been challenged by Ferdinand Lot, *The End of the Ancient World and the Beginning of the Middle Ages* (New York, 1931). Alfons Dopsch, in *The Economic and Social Foundations of European Civilization* (New York, 1937), has argued that there was unbroken cultural and economic continuity from the later Roman Empire into the Carolingian period. The thesis of Henri Pirenne's *Mohammed and Charlemagne* (London, 1939) is that such continuity was present until the Islamic conquest of the Mediterranean. Other helpful studies include R. F. Arragon's *The Transition from the Ancient to the Medieval World* (New York, 1936); H. St.-L. B. Moss, *The Birth of the Middle Ages, 395–814* (2nd ed., London, 1947); and Solomon Katz, *The Decline of Rome and the Rise of Medieval Europe* (Ithaca, 1955). Valuable contributions to the discussion have been made more recently by a collection of essays edited by Lynn White, *The Transformations of the Roman World: Gibbon's Problem after Two Centuries* (Berkeley and Los Angeles, 1966) and by Peter Brown's *The World of Late Antiquity*, A.D. *150–750* (London, 1971), an excerpt from which is included in this volume.

The literature of the various interpretations of Rome's fall is enormous. The following represents only a sampling. Some are basically political: K. J. Beloch's, "Der Verfall der antiken Kultur," *Historische Zeitschrift* 84 (1900), argues that by absorbing the Greek city-states, the Roman Empire stifled the creative forces of antiquity. E. Kornemann's "Das Problem des Untergangs der antiken Welt," *Vergangenheit und Gegenwart* 12 (1922): 193–202 and 241–54, blames Rome's fall on the reduction of the military force by Augustus. G. Ferrero, in his *La Ruine de la civilisation antique* (Paris, 1921), believes that by returning to the hereditary principle and appointing his son Commodus to the throne, Marcus Aurelius undermined the authority of the senate and the basis of the Roman state. Heitland's thesis, included here, is also political in its emphasis. He elaborated it in two subsequent pamphlets, *Iterum, or a Further Discussion of the Roman Fate* (Cambridge, 1925) and *Last Words on the Roman Municipalities* (Cambridge, 1928).

To the category of economic and social explanation belong the selections from Rostovtzeff, Walbank, Boak, and Baynes. At the center of many of such explanations is the failure of antiquity to develop modern forms of industry and economic organization. An explanation for this failure is offered by K. Bucher, *Die Entstehung der Volkwirtschaft* (16th ed., Tubingen, 1922); G. Salvioli, *Il capitalismo antico* (Bari, 1929); and M. Weber, "Wirtschaft und Gesellschaft," *Grundriss der Soziolokonomik* (1921), pp. 221 ff. They contend that ancient industry could not develop because the ancient world never emerged from the stage of house-economy to the heights of city-economy and state-economy. Their position is challenged by Rostovtzeff in his article, "The Decay of the Ancient World and Its Economic Explanation," *Economic History Review* 2 (1939): 197 ff. In the same category would fall the theory of V. G. Simkhovitch, "Rome's Fall Reconsidered," *Political Science Quarterly* 31 (1916): 201–43, presenting the argument in favor of exhaustion of the soil as a factor, and that of Ellsworth Huntington, "Climatic Change and Agricultural Exhaustion as Elements in the Fall of Rome," *Quarterly Journal of Economics* 31 (February 1917): 173 ff. The economic experiences of the twentieth century have given rise to some other economic suggestions for Rome's fall, such as L. C. West's in "The Economic Collapse of the Roman Empire," *Classical Journal* 26 (1931): 96 ff., and W. D. Gray, "The Roman Depression and Our Own," *Classical Journal* 29 (1934): 243 ff.

Various interpretations of a biological nature have also been put forth. Tenney Frank's essay, "Race Mixture in the Roman Empire," *American Historical Review* 21 (July 1916): 689–708, argued that the decline of Rome resulted from "the fact that the people who built Rome had given way to a different race." The factual basis of his theory, the distribution of foreign names on Roman gravestones, has been challenged by M. L. Gordon, "The Nationality of Slaves under the Early Roman Empire," *Journal of Roman Studies* 14 (1924): 93–111. Another version of the biological explanation is that of O. Seeck, *Geschichte des Untergangs der antiken Welt* (Berlin, 1901), who sees as the cause of Rome's collapse the "extermination of the best" among its citizens by foreign and civil wars. Some, like Oswald Spengler, *The Decline of the West* (2 vols., London, 1926–1928), believe that all societies are overtaken by natural decay.

The theory that Christianity was to blame was held by many pagans who survived Alaric's sack of Rome in 410 and brought forth apologetic responses by the Christians, among them Saint Augustine. Gibbon hinted broadly at such an explanation in several passages. The idea has not won wide support, yet it keeps recurring in one form or another. An attempt to revitalize it with an injection of Marxism was made by G. Sorel, *La Ruine du monde antique* (Paris, 1925). As Rostovtzeff said, "this book is without value for the historian." Still, so sober and excellent historian as Michael Grant, in an excerpt included in this volume and elsewhere in his *The Fall of the Roman Empire: A Reappraisal* (London, 1976), argues that Christianity played an important, but not unique, role in undermining the defense of Roman culture. The study of the place of Christianity in the Roman world, therefore, remains important. Valuable contributions to this field include: M. L. W. Laistner, *Christianity and Pagan Culture in the Later Roman Empire* (Ithaca, 1951); E. A. Goodenough, *The Church in the Roman Empire* (New York, 1931); A. Momigliano, ed., *The Conflict between Paganism and Christianity* (Oxford, 1963); E. R. Dodds, *Pagan and Christian in an Age of Anxiety* (Cambridge, 1965). Peter Brown's *Augustine of Hippo* is a particularly valuable study of a key figure.

Arnold Toynbee treats the problem of Rome's decline in the fourth volume of his *A Study of History* (Oxford, 1936), where he deals with the problem of decline in general. A more recent book by R. M. Haywood, *The Myth of Rome's Fall* (New York, 1958), returns to something like Bury's view. To the questions, "Can we learn something of the future by our study of the Roman Empire? Will that study not yield some great secret of civilization?" Haywood answers "No." We may expect the answers only to "innumerable minor ones." However that may be, it is nonetheless necessary to continue asking the major ones.